THE COUPLE

THE

COUPLE

A Sexual Profile by Mr. and Mrs. K

As Told to Monte Ghertler and Alfred Palca

Coward, McCann & Geoghegan, Inc.
NEW YORK

Copyright © 1971 by Monte Ghertler and Alfred Palca

All rights reserved. This book, or parts thereof, may not be reproduced in any form without permission in writing from the publisher. Published simultaneously in Canada by Longmans Canada Limited, Toronto.

Library of Congress Catalog Card Number: 70-146079

PRINTED IN THE UNITED STATES OF AMERICA

In early 1970 we were patients at the Reproductive Biology Research Foundation in St. Louis. Between August 1 and September 15, 1970 we put our memories of the experience on tape. We were patients, not trained medical observers or scientists. Our book is based on our memory of events more than a year old now.

Our reason for writing it is that we have had an experience so unusual and, for us, significant, that despite our lack of training, we feel the story deserves to be told. We also hope that it will give information and encouragement to others with sexual problems.

We have changed some names, places, background material and conversations, but in essence this is our story.

Mr. and Mrs. K
January, 1971

THE COUPLE

LOS ANGELES

JANUARY, 1970

HAROLD

The price seems crazy.

First comes the $2,500 you pay Masters and Johnson.

Next, you've got to get there. In our case that would mean another $450. Then, figure maybe an additional thousand for hotels, food, car, cabs, gifts, phone calls.

It could add up to about $4,000 or a nearly unbelievable $300 a day.

A total of $300 a day for two weeks and, believe me, it's no vacation. You don't go to a glamorous sanitorium in the Alps. You don't go to a restful estate overlooking the Pacific. It all takes place in St. Louis, Missouri.

And you don't get any guarantees either. You can come back in the same state you were in when you left home.

What were we hoping to cure? Cancer? A psychosis? Nothing that bad. All we had was something that ninety percent of the married couples in America occasionally suffer from. We just had it worse. It hurt, but as far as I know, it's never killed anyone.

But it would have killed our marriage for sure. And if I'd lost Joan, I have a feeling my future sex life would have been one hundred percent prostitutes or masturbation.

I'd reached a point where normal sex, with a person that mattered to me, meant frustration every single time.

JOAN

To be aroused to a point of excitement and then left hanging there and to have it happen again and again, and to know it's never going to be any different, is a very special torture.

We'd sought help for years from doctors, psychiatrists, and marriage counsellors. But we never stayed with any of them very long. Their treatments never seemed to get anywhere, so we'd lose heart or just get bored. Harold, for example, has had five different psychiatrists, but the longest he ever stayed with one was seven weeks.

After nine years of marriage, we had pretty well resigned ourselves to a divorce or to a life of unsatisfactory sex or no sex at all. I don't know if we even loved each other anymore. We said we did, but our fights were getting worse and worse, and we sure couldn't make up in bed the way other people probably do.

The cost of Masters and Johnson? Well, when you think that we found the money to fix my teeth when that was necessary, or to put Barbara through college and then pay for her wedding last October, or to give Harold's father a seventieth birthday party, well, then this money could be found, too. What price can you put on a marriage?

I was in bed wearing earphones last night, with the radio tuned to a late-night talk show. Suddenly a man on the program said something about an *erection* and I came to attention.

". . . and almost the moment he achieves penetration, he has an orgasm," the fellow said, and I thought, well, it's a lively one tonight. I looked over and saw Harold was sleeping already.

"This kind of case," the man said, "is known as premature ejaculation, a problem that is far more prevalent than any of us realize. Men become so sexually aroused that they are unable to sustain their erections long enough to bring their partners to climax. The new Masters and Johnson book, *Human Sexual Inadequacy*, will discuss this problem when it is published in the spring of this year."

It was January, 1970. I made a mental note to buy the book.

"Most astonishing," the man on the radio continued, "is that Masters and Johnson have been curing cases of premature ejaculation—and impotence—and frigidity—and doing it in fourteen days!"

Come on, I thought to myself, he has got to be kidding. Fourteen days for a sex problem? Harold and I had been going to doctors for years, and the problem was worse today than ever. How could they talk about cures in only fourteen days? I figured they had to be quacks.

The man on the program was a doctor who had written a magazine article about Masters and Johnson. He was positive their work would one day compare with Freud's. I stayed awake and listened until two o'clock in the morning.

When I woke up, Harold had left, so I called him at the

store and told him what I'd heard. He said if I wanted to find out about getting the treatment it was all right with him. I said I wasn't sure how to go about it, but I'd see what I could do.

I phoned the radio station, and they gave me an address and telephone number, which turned out to be in St. Louis, and since I really hate to write letters—I'm better when I can talk—I figured I'd try to call. A receptionist in St. Louis answered.

"I'm calling long distance from Los Angeles. I want to talk to someone about coming for treatment."

"One moment, please."

The next thing I heard was a woman's voice saying, "Dr. Schumacher speaking."

I told her why I was calling, and she asked me who recommended us and exactly what the problem was. I told her, and then asked if they really had as good a record of cures as the man on the radio had said.

"Yes, it's rather good," she said. "Of course we don't promise success, but—"

"Oh, we don't expect guarantees," I assured her. "We're willing to take our chances. When can we have an appointment?"

"I couldn't possibly tell you now on the phone. I suggest you write and ask for an appointment. I imagine it can be arranged for some time in May or June."

"May or June?" I know my voice was shaking like I was going to cry or get hysterical. "Look, Dr. Schumacher," I said, "we really have a desperate situation here. We're at the point now . . . I mean this is such an emergency . . . I . . . we can't last till May. We've been married for nine years and we're at the breaking point . . . We need help very badly."

She must have sensed how things were with us because,

after a little pause, she suddenly asked me, "When did you have your last period?" I was surprised at this, but I told her, and she said she would call me back.

In fifteen minutes I was called by a Miss Bowen who said that Dr. Schumacher had turned the matter over to her. She said she had managed to find two open dates, January 26 and February 2. Since the January date would conflict with my period, could we come to St. Louis for our two weeks of treatment starting February 2?

"Let me check with my husband," I said.

I told Harold about my conversations with St. Louis and that they could see us in three weeks. Could he get away that soon? He told me to hold the phone for a minute, and when he got back he said yes. I dialed St. Louis again and told Miss Bowen that we'd be able to come.

"Good," she said. "Now where would you like to stay? You can have either apartment or hotel accommodations. The apartment is one hundred a week and you can do your own cooking, the hotel's a hundred and fifty."

I said I'd rather not do any cooking, and she said she didn't blame me. "Incidentally," I asked, "is there any fee?"

She said, "Fee? Yes. It's twenty-five hundred dollars."

I nearly sank down into our basement. Twenty-five hundred dollars for two weeks of medical treatment? I'd never heard of such a thing. I tried to play it cool with Miss Bowen, but I was shocked. I knew the $2,500 was only the beginning—add transportation and food and taxis and rooms and you'd wind up with nearly $4,000. I told her I'd have to call my husband again. I was pretty sure he'd say no.

But you can never tell about Harold. When you expect him to be excited, he's very calm. All he said was okay, if you think it can do any good, tell them we'll come to St. Louis.

HAROLD

January 19

I'd heard of Masters and Johnson before Joan called me at the store. In fact, one of my doctors had recommended them in a halfhearted way.

"I've been *told* their treatments have been somewhat successful," he said. He had no idea "how" they did it, and the subject hadn't come up again.

My own information about Masters and Johnson was sketchy to say the least. As I understood it:

(1) Instead of asking questions like Kinsey, they watched people making love and took films;
(2) they measured penises, clitorises, and vaginas;
(3) they ran a clinic in a university where people gave each other rubdowns before having sex;
(4) one of them was a woman.

Their first book had already been published, but I hadn't read it. My facts probably came from *Time* or *The Reader's Digest*. I had the impression Masters and Johnson were the most important thing to happen to sex since Kinsey.

Joan mentioned one thing that really excited me, though:

the two weeks. She thought it was short. To me it sounded long. Two solid weeks of twenty-four-hour-a-day sexual therapy! There was a new idea. I'd heard of twenty-four-hour-a-day therapy for dope addiction, nervous breakdowns, alcoholism. Maybe—please God, just maybe—these two people had something to help this penis of mine.

I felt I owed it to Joan to try anything reasonable. If you think that I missed proper intercourse, imagine how she felt. This is no nun. This is an extremely sensuous person. I could feel her enthusiasm over the telephone. It was as if she were saying to me, "Please, Harold, please take me to St. Louis. I want to get laid." Who could say no if there was even the slightest possibility this would work?

I have to admit the $2,500 shocked me. I had expected it to be free. As a matter of fact, I even imagined they might pay us. I thought we'd be part of an experimental program—like rats or college students. I had no idea that Masters and Johnson had been at it for more than thirteen years and had already treated hundreds of couples successfully. Luckily, I could afford it.

Besides, as my mother used to say, "What good is money if you don't have your health." I don't suppose Mama included being a good lay in her definition of health, but I assure you, a sexual problem is a disease. If you've got one, you suffer humiliation every time you have sex. You're told sex is life's big thrill, and you're denied it. If you're single, you avoid sexual encounters. If you're married, you wonder how your wife can stand you. You try to hide behind disguises. You build up muscles, talk tough, jog, wear rough clothes. You've seen those signs that say, ALCOHOLISM IS A DISEASE. Compared to my problem, alcoholism is a *mitzva*.

JOAN

January 20

  Making love with Harold was usually like this: I'd be in the kitchen, say, and he'd come in and grab me and give me one of those caveman kisses of his. He was normally a rough person, and whenever he'd kiss me it was very forceful, very strong. It was never something that was gentle and pleasant. I could always feel his erection between my legs, pushing into me through my dress, and when I'd feel it, I'd get hot even though I knew what was going to happen.
  We'd stay there for a little while, kissing and rubbing against each other, and then he'd sort of lead me into the bedroom. By the time we'd get there—which in our house takes maybe five seconds—his erection would be gone, and my excitement would fly out the window. Anyhow, we'd both take off our clothes, and when we were naked, Harold would grab me again. Maybe he'd manage a half-erection, and then we'd kiss nude; it would get slightly harder, and I'd get hot again, too. So I'd take it in my hand and try to guide it into me, but nine times out of ten it would go down before I could get it in me and he'd have that embarrassed smile on his face and say something like, "Try rubbing it."
  Well, this *always* turned me off, but I'd feel sorry for him,

and I'd try to give him an erection with my hand, but that hardly ever worked. So I'd slip down and put it in my mouth and try to get it hard that way. Once in a while he'd get a partial erection while his penis was in my mouth, and then he'd quickly take it out and try to get it inside while it was still hard. And sometimes it would work. He'd get it all the way in and wham!—he'd come right away. I liked to feel him come inside me, but I'd rarely have an orgasm that way.

Usually, though, even sucking didn't give him an erection, but if I kept it up long enough he would come in my mouth. I always thought it was pretty strange that he could come without an erection, but he could. It wouldn't get me aroused, though, because without an erection it seemed like nothing.

That's how it was for seven years. I felt awfully sorry for him. And then I started feeling sorry for myself. I felt like I was being used like a machine.

HAROLD

January 20

    The moment I'd get an erection, I'd want to jump right on top of Joan and make love. So I'd kiss her real hard, but the minute I started putting it into her the same old fears would start. Right away my mind would say, "You've got to satisfy her," or "You better produce this time," and then ninety percent of the time I would lose the erection. I'd try to get it back by rubbing against her or by having her play with my penis or by getting her to suck it. I'd get partial erections, but usually I'd just lose them.
    Well, of course, each time it happened I'd lose faith in myself and start feeling terrible about Joan. I'd be afraid that she'd become frigid—which at one time she did—or perhaps that she'd go look elsewhere. That was always in the back of my mind.
    The more I worried the less chance I had of keeping it up. Most of the time she tried to reassure me. She'd say things like, "Don't worry . . . don't worry . . ." and then I'd usually be able to come. Sometimes I'd come in her mouth even without an erection and sometimes I'd be able to get inside

HAROLD: *January 20*

and come there. After I'd come, I'd feel ashamed because I knew I hadn't performed like a man.

And she didn't always reassure me. Sometimes she'd just get mad about the whole thing, and we'd go to sleep with no one talking at all. It's awful when you can't satisfy a woman.

JOAN

January 23

Four days after the phone call, a letter from Masters and Johnson arrived confirming our reservations. It contained two questionnaires, one for Harold and one for me, asking for some of our sexual background, and giving these instructions:

> *Since we are primarily interested in your individual responses, it is important that husband and wife answer questions independently of each other; that is, do not discuss your answers with each other before completing your own questionnaire.*

It's really kind of odd that someone with my attitudes about sex should be married to a man with problems like Harold's. Before we met I was one of the most promiscuous girls around. It's the only word for it. I am also what you call "orgasmic," a word picked up from one of our doctors. Extremely orgasmic. I come quickly, violently, and often. Absolutely normal in that respect. If there's an opposite to frigid, I'm it.

But even before I heard of orgasms I liked sex. In my teens

I never masturbated to climax, but masturbating was pleasant, as were my first tries at intercourse. It wasn't till I was seventeen that a young law student showed me what I was missing.

I had a job in an ice cream factory in Compton and met a Jewish boy who was working his way through UCLA. We went to bed together and afterward he asked me if I'd had an orgasm. I said I didn't know what that was. He tried to explain it to me. I was really surprised.

"You mean girls are supposed to finish up like boys?"

He smiled. I think he thought I might be kidding him. "And enjoy themselves as much," he said. "At least more than you've been doing."

He promised to help me have an orgasm. What a revelation. It wasn't that he was such a great lover, but he used psychology. Up until then men had simply wanted me to do things for them, never asking me what I wanted or liked. I was flattered when this fellow seemed to be considerate and interested in me. That was half of it, I think. And when I told him it sometimes hurt when the penis was going in, he smeared his with vaseline and put some in my vagina. For the first time the penetration felt slippery and nice.

When he was in me, lying on top, he said, "Now feel it down inside you. Hold it and roll it around. Play with it, Joan, enjoy it." That sounded wild to me. I tried to understand what he meant. "Come on," he said, "move around with me."

He was getting aroused. He started moving his penis inside me slowly and kissing me on the breast. And for once, instead of being just a spectator, I was being urged to take part, too. I began to feel how nice it was to have a penis inside me. My breath started coming faster.

"Don't hold back now, Joan," he gasped. "Really let it come."

He didn't have to tell me. I no longer had control. I came with a yell, and it was beautiful. I couldn't wait to have more.

Most women say they need a deep, meaningful relationship before they can experiment with sex. In those days I wasn't like that. I lived pretty wild and free. I had run away from Fresno at fourteen to come to Los Angeles to live with one of my sisters. In a year I ran away from her to take a place of my own. I had no family supervision, and at sixteen I looked like a woman of twenty-two and started behaving like one, or how I *thought* they behaved.

I was pretty and found it easy to attract men. Now that sex had become more pleasurable I found myself doing it more often. I left my hangups in Fresno, and though I had to like a fellow before I went to bed with him, I didn't need an engagement ring.

My real education in sex and my introduction to a world of culture and learning came when I got a job as a messenger in the mail room of a movie studio on Melrose Avenue. I worked there over two years, and my studio sex education started with greedy assistant directors who had a lot of power among the less important people at the studio. Any pretty girl who wanted to make it in pictures generally started with the assistant directors.

But I found out pretty quickly I really wasn't interested in an acting career. I was much more attracted to the writers on the lot. Not that I wanted to write myself, but I liked their jokes and their culture and their intelligence. And when they found that I was anxious to learn about all sorts of different things, they gave me books to read, took me to concerts and museums, and more or less gave me an education.

I realized, of course, that most of them just wanted to sleep with me, but I was just as interested in sleeping with them. And at least they could talk to me about books and art and ideas instead of just sex and the movie business like the assistant directors. They gave me an interest in culture that has lasted all through my life. And one of them told me a story that made me feel better about my constant readiness to go to bed with the scriptwriters. He said that when Dylan Thomas lectured at Cambridge, all the girls at Radcliffe tried to get laid by him, and Thomas slept with as many as he could handle. So those college girls were just like me, except they wanted to make it with a poet instead of a screenwriter.

My friend gave me a book Thomas wrote, and I still have it. It got me interested in poetry, and to this day I read it once in a while. Very few people today know that I never got past the seventh grade in school.

My main subject at that time was sex, though, and I guess I tried almost everything during my years at the studio. But when I left I was more confused than ever. I still liked sex, but the popular songs and the movies talked a lot about love, which was something that never came up in my relationships with assistant directors and writers.

HAROLD

January 23

It took Joan an hour to fill out her questionnaire. I did mine in five minutes. I guess that tells it all. Although my sexual *problem* has dominated my life, my sexual *experience* is nearly zero. Do you know how many women, outside of prostitutes, I've had? Three—and two of them wives.

I've had so little sexual contact that you'd think I grew up in a small town in Iowa. But I'm from Los Angeles. You know, car hops, Black Dahlias, casting couches. Not that my Los Angeles is Hedda Hopper's. We came here in the thirties and settled in a district called Beverly Fairfax where my father opened a small furniture store. I'm in the business now, and we do pretty well. But once we were so poor that I was almost the only boy in Fairfax High who didn't even *try* to get into college.

At Fairfax I belonged to a group of boys so awkward and unsophisticated it was hard to believe any of us would ever get laid. Yet, despite the odds, that was all we ever thought about. Some chance. How was Nate W., who looked like a rabbit and took corrective gym, going to get laid? Or Alan P. with pimples like doorknobs. Our one hope was Bob B. who was practically handsome and acted older than the rest of us. As a matter of fact, he'd already had a major sexual triumph in the balcony of the Normandy Theater. To this day I can remember his story almost word for word.

"I was up there concentrating on the movie when a woman sat down next to me. When she lit a cigarette, I could see that while she wasn't young, she seemed very available. I could swear she was looking for it. So I got a big hard-on and began to pray for enough nerve to speak to her when—get this—without a word, she took my hand, slipped it under her dress and guided it straight to her pussy. There I was, fingerfucking a lady I'd never spoken a word to."

His story got me so hot that it supplied me with material for months of masturbation. It also meant that for years I sat only in the theater balconies. Orchestras were for nuns and tourists. In the balcony there was always hope.

Our lives were run by sexual rumor. If we heard of a pick-up in a roller rink, we'd spend every evening on skates. Were whores reported in McArthur Park? Night after night we circled the area leaning out of Nate W.'s car making nearly inaudible remarks to any woman walking alone.

One day Bob B. actually found the real thing. "It's *real* nookie this time kid. Three dollars. I've phoned. I've got the address. I told her four o'clock."

The apartment was above a funeral parlor in Santa Monica which turned Bob B. instantly philosophical: "Life ends on street level Harold, but begins one flight up."

The girl was beautiful, a little old, but beautiful. An Okie Greer Garson. A short conference produced this news. "For three dollars I only suck." *Only?* The *word* was almost enough. "Terrific. Who's arguing? Who's first?"

The woman chose me.

I'll be brief—as brief as the experience. When we got into the other room, she said, "Let me wash you off." There was a sink in a corner. She held my penis in her hand and said, "What a nice one."

Three dollars went down the sink.

Waiting in the car for Bob I thought to myself, *Here I am seventeen and my only sexual contacts have been two pairs of hands: mine and now hers.* It remained that way until I met Myra, my first wife.

HAROLD

February 1

We were standing in the stockroom after closing the store. Papa looked at me as if I were crazy.

"St. Louis? [a pause while he places it] St. Louis, *Missouri?* [that seemed to make it worse] Two *weeks* in St. Louis, Missouri? Who's in St. Louis? What's in St. Louis? Why would anybody go to St. Louis?"

Let's face it, those are reasonable questions. I challenge anyone to explain two weeks in St. Louis. What can you say—that you've always dreamed of touring the Budweiser Brewery?

I suppose most people who are going there to see Masters and Johnson simply tell friends and relations something like, "We're going to St. Louis on business." Or else they tell the truth. But my business is the family business, so I couldn't use that. And I didn't feel like telling my folks the truth because I didn't feel like telling them the truth. I can't remember ever having a frank discussion about sex with them, and forty-two seemed a little late to begin.

I'd never tried to picture their sex life, and I assumed they never thought of mine. Actually, when I was living at home the idea that the two of them might be at it would flash across my mind every February 3, their anniversary. "People probably do it on their anniversary," I'd think, and instantly try to think of other things. But I couldn't keep it out. "Could it be that right now, in that room, those two . . ." Another voice inside me would practically shout, "Stop, you pervert." My big fear was that I would begin to picture them banging away and that I'd masturbate while thinking of Mama and Papa. Even I couldn't be that depraved.

Surprisingly, a week or so after we returned from St. Louis we *were* able to tell my father the truth, or at least try to. That, in itself, is a tribute to Masters and Johnson. I learned that people wouldn't despise me because of a sexual problem.

I said, "Pop, do you know why we went to St. Louis? To visit a place that treats sex problems."

"You could have told me that before you left," he said, "I would have understood."

Maybe. Do you know, that's all he said. He didn't ask *what* the problem was. He didn't ask *whose* problem it was. He didn't even ask if it had been cured.

The story we cooked up for the folks was pretty incredible, if you know anything about American geography. Fortunately, neither of them do. We told them we were going to St. Louis for the winter sports.

We told my brother the truth, because my mother had been having serious headaches for more than a year and had been in the hospital twice. We wanted to be sure that someone in the family would be able to reach us immediately if anything happened. When I told Miltie about Masters and Johnson, he said, "Oh boy, lead me to it." Later I realized it was not such a joke.

One of our doctors was excited. "You're medical pioneers," he said, "like Freud's early patients."

* * *

HAROLD: *February 1*

On the plane Joan said that the man on the radio that night claimed that Masters and Johnson achieve high rates of cure because patients arrive there with so much faith in them.

" 'Prior trust' is what I think he called it," she said.

I think this is unquestionably true. We'd done some reading about Masters and Johnson before leaving, and we realized that we were about to meet two extraordinary scientists.

Before Masters and Johnson, nobody had ever looked at sex scientifically. All the information had been second hand. For example, doctors didn't really know whether or not it was safe to have sex during pregnancy until Masters and Johnson actually observed what happened to the fetus during intercourse. To do this they used a clear plastic penis which allowed them to photograph the insides of a woman's vagina, even to make color movies there. The plastic penis, which is powered by a small motor, duplicates a man's motions. It can be adjusted for speed of thrust, direction, depth. Its size can be altered to fit any woman. It even has a device which lets it shoot out real sperm or other fluids.

They were also the first to take a look at a diaphragm during intercourse and could see why it sometimes failed, and they used similar techniques to observe the action and evaluate other birth control devices.

Masters and Johnson proved that the size and location of a clitoris has no relationship to a woman's ability to have orgasms.

They also demonstrated that a woman can have multiple orgasms and that the size of a man's penis has nothing to do with the quality of his performance.

They studied sexual responses in old people and found no time limit to female sexuality and that men in their eighties can enjoy sex too.

They've made great advances in the study of infertility, too. By using the plastic penis, they've actually been able to watch semen fertilize an egg inside a woman's vagina.

I'm normally a pessimist, but there's no denying that my reading gave me a lot of "prior trust."

The plane was nearly full, and I found myself wondering, "What *are* all these people going to St. Louis for?"

ST. LOUIS

FEBRUARY, 1970

JOAN

Sunday Night

The taxi from the airport took us to a section of St. Louis called Forest Park, which was where the clinic was located. We rode into the compound of the Barnes Hospital and stopped at a building with a canopy. In the lobby a desk clerk confirmed our reservation and took us up to our rooms.

We seemed to be in some sort of combined hospital and hotel, and this was evidently the hotel section with thick carpets and subdued lighting. Our suite looked out on a skating rink in a beautiful park, and consisted of a bedroom, dressing room and bath, all very nicely furnished. In the elevator on our way out to dinner we saw doctors and nurses in whites, patients in bathrobes, and people like us who seemed to be guests.

I was sort of nervous and distracted that evening. If this St. Louis trip didn't work, Harold and I were finished, which would be such a mess I didn't even want to think about it. Maybe I should have left things the way they were. They weren't good, but at least they were going along. Now they could fall apart completely.

I talked Harold into spending all this money, even though he did okay every move we made. If this failed, our fights would be worse than ever and it would be my fault. The trouble with sex problems is, if you're not satisfied in that department, you're going to take it out in other ways. Some people say wars come from frustrated horny men trying to make up for what they can't manage in bed, and I can see how that might be possible. Harold and I had our worst fights because of failures in sex.

So I was distracted as we drove to Stan Musial's restaurant for dinner, and I didn't notice much of St. Louis except The Arch which the cab driver, the hotel clerk, the doorman, and the waiter told us we *had* to see because it's St. Louis' answer to the Eiffel Tower and the Statue of Liberty. Well, I don't know anything about art, so all I can say is, Good Luck to you, St. Louis.

After dinner we decided it was too cold to walk, and everything was closed because it was Sunday night, so we caught a taxi back to the hotel. As soon as I got into the hot tub, I realized how exhausted I was from the tension and nervousness of the day, the good-byes and the arrangements, the last-minute packing, the plane trip, the worries about whether the whole thing was a mistake or not.

I got into bed and turned on the TV while Harold took his bath. Seeing the same rotten programs in St. Louis that we had in LA made me feel at home, though it was funny to watch local commercials for markets or department stores I'd never heard of.

When Harold finally came out of the bathroom, I was lying on my side with my head on the pillow and my back to the bathroom. Something told me that when he got into bed he was going to snuggle up to me, and sure enough he did. I wasn't sure what to do. We hadn't had sex, normal or otherwise, for a long time because I'd refused to have a life of nothing but oral sex. Now Harold evidently wanted to try one more time in the hope that, by some miracle, he wouldn't need any treatment and we'd be able to tell them in the morning we were going back home to LA, cured.

I knew there wasn't much hope of that. But if we tried and failed we'd probably have a terrible argument, and if we didn't try we'd probably have a terrible argument. I didn't know what to do. Our fights were awful. Sometimes when I screamed at him he would tell me I was going crazy, really losing my mind. He knew I worried about that. My father and sisters had all been in institutions, two of them chronic alcoholics, another a paranoid wreck who tried to kill herself.

Of course I didn't just sit and take it, I gave back as good as I got. But no matter how violent the battles, we hung on to each other, I can't really understand why. Maybe we loved each other, whatever that means, or maybe we just didn't want to hurt his parents, an old Jewish couple who wouldn't talk to me or come to our wedding because I was a wild *shiksa*. Now they considered me their closest daughter and would be heartbroken if anything happened to separate me and Harold.

But now Harold was rubbing against me and pushing his penis between my legs from the rear and reaching around to cup my breasts in his hand.

"My legs feel so weak, hon," he whispered, and I smiled. It was an old joke between us, his kidding way of getting me to feel sorry for him, an indirect request for kisses and caresses to make him whole and strong. "Really, I'm not kidding," he said, "they're very, very weak."

I felt a kind of warmth and love I hadn't experienced for a while. I turned around and kissed him, and our naked bodies touching aroused us both a little. He had his penis lying in my crotch, and I suddenly realized he had a partial erection and that I was getting hot. It had been such a long time; I wondered if this was the season for miracles and St. Louis was America's Lourdes.

He mounted me and tried to get his penis inside. In a minute we were right back where we started. Nothing. Neither of us said a word. For a long time Harold just lay there on top of me, that terrible, grim look on his face, and I knew the guilts he was having, how he'd let me down as a husband and what a failure he was as a man.

The thing is, I'd gotten used to those failures over the years, and that was why I'd stopped letting myself get aroused, until I reached the point where I wasn't even sure I had any sex interest left. The letdowns and disappointments were too awful. Yet here I'd let myself get excited again and nothing was going to happen. I made up my mind I wouldn't get angry, though. It hadn't worked and that was that. Tomorrow we'd go to the clinic and hope that they could help us.

I was going to say this to Harold when I realized that he was whispering something to me. I took his face in my hands.

"What did you say?" I asked softly.

"Kiss it for me, hon."

I swear I wanted to cry. *Nothing had changed at all.* Nothing was going to change. This trip was a waste of time and money. If I had my choice, that minute we'd have dressed and gone right home.

HAROLD

Sunday Night

Regret hit me seconds before I ejaculated. Sad when you think about it. A man about to have an orgasm having regrets instead of enjoying himself. I wondered how to report the incident to Masters and Johnson. I wanted to get it just right. Self-pity and all. I was studying myself hard that evening, trying to notice small details that might be useful the next day. I'd done the same thing with psychiatrists: "I must remember that dream exactly. Maybe it contains *the clue.*"

I'd had a semi-erection all right. It had risen when Joan climbed into bed. When I pressed against her, it had actually *stayed* semi-hard. When I rolled on top of her, I really thought I might get it in.

Arrivederci, hard-on.

Do you know why it shriveled up? Believe it or not, because of the desk clerk.

"I wonder if he knows why we're here," I'd whispered to Joan after we registered.

"How could he?" she said.

"Well, Masters and Johnson made the reservation. He must know who they make reservations for."

31

"Don't be silly," she said. "Besides, they may think it's me. Frigid, or something."

So right there, on top of Joan, I began worrying about the desk clerk again. Not a big worry. No visions of him picking up the phone to tell everyone in the place, "He's *here!*" It was just a little worry, but enough to make me soft.

I could sense Joan's irritation. Was she annoyed because *she* was still aroused? Or because I was still aroused?

"I'm still hot," I lied. "If you suck it, I may make it."

She scooted down very eagerly. "Oh, God, she's really hot." And there's the one thought *guaranteed* to end any possibility of erection from me. A woman who needs satisfaction is my nightmare.

So we ended as I feared. I came with a soft penis.

Why had we tried it that night? Passion? New surroundings? Was I just rechecking my symptoms before reporting them? Was I trying to prove I didn't need Masters and Johnson? Was Joan?

Later, in a book about the clinic I read, "Every married couple, if they are speaking at all, will try to have intercourse the night before they see us, just to see if they can."

JOAN

Monday Morning

At the address for the clinic I expected to find a sign saying MASTERS AND JOHNSON or something. Instead it said REPRODUCTIVE BIOLOGY RESEARCH FOUNDATION, which turned out to be the clinic's full name. Inside the white colonial-style building a receptionist phoned upstairs and then told us to take the elevator to the second floor. Men and women of the staff were walking around in white pants and smocks, and we were shown to a waiting room that had chairs and magazines like a thousand other medical offices. I don't know what we expected. Harold and I were too nervous to read, so we talked a little about what we thought might happen, but I had a crazy idea that the vases or lamps in the room might conceal a "bug" recording our entire conversation.

In a few minutes a door opened and a woman took us into a nearby office which actually did have a microphone on the desk. She gave us some typed sheets of paper which listed restaurants, museums, theaters, sports activities, and other entertainment facilities in St. Louis, then excused herself.

She returned in a minute and said, "Dr. Masters and Mrs. Johnson will see you now."

We gave each other surprised looks as we followed her

down the hall. Miss Bowen had said that patients were treated by a team consisting of a man and woman, but that Dr. Masters and Mrs. Johnson would probably be too busy to handle us themselves and that we'd get one of the other three couples on the staff. Before we could make any comment, we were shown into an office where a man and woman were standing behind a desk. The man was Dr. Masters, and he introduced himself and Mrs. Johnson, and they shook our hands. He was very businesslike.

"This will be a brief meeting, Mr. and Mrs. K.," he said, "to introduce ourselves and tell you something about our procedure. This morning Mr. K. will come with me for a ninety-minute interview, while Mrs. K stays here with Mrs. Johnson. Tomorrow we'll switch."

He pointed to the microphone on the desk.

"All our discussions are recorded. You may be self-conscious about this at first, I'm sure you'll get used to it quickly. The tapes are kept by us in a vault, and at the end of five years will be destroyed. Only Mrs. Johnson and I have access to them."

The fellow on the radio program had talked about this. By having the interviews taped, Masters and Johnson could concentrate on the patients and not worry about taking notes. Then at another time they could listen to each other's tapes if necessary.

"On Wednesday morning you will be given physical examinations," he continued, "then the four of us will meet for a roundtable discussion. At that time you will be given your first instructions in the treatment. Until then I will ask each of you not to talk with each other about the history-taking sessions."

We nodded.

"One last thing. No intercourse or any other sexual activity until authorized by Mrs. Johnson or me."

JOAN: *Monday Morning*

Before I could nod again he was shaking my hand and leading Harold to the door. "Nice to meet you, Mrs. K., I'll see you tomorrow morning."

They closed the door. I turned, and for the first time really, looked at Mrs. Johnson. The man on the radio had said she was divorced and had a child. I took her to be fortyish and rather attractive. She, too, wore a white smock over her dress, no makeup, and her hair was very casual, as though she'd just gotten up from sleep and run a comb through it. She gave me a warm smile.

"How was your trip from Los Angeles?" she asked. "Are you pleased with your living accommodations? If not we'll arrange for others."

Mrs. Johnson is the kind of person who can ask questions like that as though she's genuinely interested and will really do something if you're not happy. Somehow we were soon talking about children to my surprise, and she said she had a confession to make.

"I have a very lovely daughter," she said, "who has her own horse but he's rather old and she wants a new one. Well, I'm ashamed to say I've just made a deal with her. I know I shouldn't, it's against what I stand for, but I had to bribe her because she's started smoking. I told her if she stopped I'd get her the horse. Do you think that's awful of me?"

I laughed. I've done much worse with Harold's daughter Barbara from his first marriage, and often. But it immediately put us on a woman to woman basis, and for a while we talked children. I found her one of the warmest and most charming people I'd ever met. In a matter of minutes I was telling her about myself and my marriage as I might to a life-long friend. She asked particularly about my attitude toward my husband. I told her, "Well, here, Mrs. Johnson," I said, "we come to what I wrote in the application. My husband spends far more time with his family than he ever does with me. In fact, he thinks more of everyone in the world than he does of me. Everyone. I'm a second-class citizen. They all come ahead of me. And frankly I resent it. I resent it very much."

I told it all, the fights, the heartbreaks, the works. She was very nice but didn't make many comments. I tried to be honest because for $2,500 I'd be crazy to fool around. I also told her about my first husband.

Not that there's much to tell. I fell for a pretty face, that's all. It was a couple of years after I left the studio and I had a job demonstrating makeup at the May Company. Paul was an able-bodied seaman in the merchant marine, and when he came to call for me, every girl in the store stopped work to look at him, he was that handsome. He was fairly good in bed, but we didn't get to do it too often because he was away at sea so much. Still I thought I loved him and swore to be faithful during those times, even though we never seriously talked about marriage. But everything about him seemed romantic, and I guess my vow was, too. I took it seriously for three years.

We finally married when he had one of his shore leaves, and then three months later I discovered that he was a fairy. A full-fledged homosexual. He came home one night with a young boy, and the two of them got undressed and had a night of sex. They kissed and embraced and caressed each other, and they had each other orally and rectally. What really knocked me out, though, was they wanted me to watch. But after a while they were so involved in each other that I managed to sneak into the living room and go to sleep on the sofa.

All right, what do you do or say when you find you've been that wrong? In the morning I told him we were finished. You know what he said? Why rock the boat? He couldn't see why we were finished. What was wrong with liking boys? Why divorce?

I looked at Mrs. Johnson. That's exactly what he told me, I said. She shook her head sympathetically. I told her how I tried to explain to Paul why it couldn't work.

"Look," I said, "I'm very broad-minded. To each his own, I'm all for that, you have whatever you like. But not on my time." In a month, I had a Mexican divorce.

"What did you do after that?" Mrs. Johnson asked.

"I went into a tailspin. I didn't go out at all. I felt that I was the one who'd been the fool, and I stayed in the house a lot. I gave up sex completely. About like now."

"What's it like for you, not having sex?"

I hesitated a minute, then figured, what the hell: "I satisfy myself by masturbating a lot."

"What do you call a lot?"

"Well, recently I've been doing it three, four times a day. Of course there are periods, though, when I don't do it for weeks. It depends on how I feel."

I'd started when I was a girl the way everyone does, and I remember in the beginning I used to think about my father's penis, which I'd seen once when I was seven or eight. I hated the man, but he was my favorite fantasy.

During my teens, when I got turned on to sex by my UCLA boyfriend, I was so orgasmic that I could come at the damnedest times and places. I did it once on a Wilshire Boulevard bus, while a good-looking fellow across the aisle flirted with me. I sort of wiggled my thighs together and rubbed myself against my purse, which I held between my legs where no one could see what I was doing. It was easier at home, though, where I sometimes did it standing or lying in front of a full-length mirror.

In that time after Paul, though, I figured out the ideal form of masturbation, a way that was often better for me than some men. I got an electric vibrator, the kind that fits right over your hand, and then I'd lie down naked in bed. The only other equipment I needed was a fantasy and a desire, and those I had most of the time. Sometimes I'd think of a strange man making love to me, either begging me to take off my clothes or else ripping them off my back. Sometimes I'd think of wild things like two men making love to me at the same time, and sometimes the idea of a woman would pop into my head.

When I was ready I'd plug in the vibrator, and instantly my hand vibrated hundreds of times a second. Then I'd put my middle finger inside my vagina, or run it along my labia or use it on my clitoris. The sensation can't be described, it's something you have to feel. At the same time I'd fondle one breast with my other hand until I felt ready to come, and then I'd grab the breast real tight. A vibrator is terrific. I've had incredible orgasms with it, orgasms that came in thirty seconds, sometimes even less.

I did tell Mrs. Johnson that I was really a little ashamed of the masturbating thing, though. She waved her hand dismissively: "It's better to get rid of sexual tensions than keep them bottled up."

I could have talked my heart out to her all day, but she stopped me after an hour and a half, because it was time for her next patient.

When I left, Harold was waiting. We put on our coats and walked out of the building together, dying to ask each other what happened. But we knew we shouldn't and didn't. The only thing Harold said was that he thought Dr. Masters was very formal and professional, but I really raved about how nice Mrs. Johnson was. I couldn't say enough about how much I liked her.

Nine days later I found out what a bitch she can be. And I mean a real bitch.

HAROLD

Monday Morning

My first impression of Dr. Masters wasn't encouraging. In fact, I began our talk by saying, "It's going to be hard getting information out of me. I don't remember a lot of things."

His handshake had put me off slightly. It seemed *too* firm, as if he was demonstrating how strong and serious he was. And the thing about his eyes. Here **was a** completely ordinary-looking man of about fifty, short, bald, pale, nothing unusual except for eyes that were absolutely scary. I think the condition is called wall-eyed, where one eye stares straight at you while the other one seems to be looking away across the room. It throws you at first, because you aren't sure that all of him is really with you.

And then the voice. Dr. Masters is a mumbler. He speaks in a low, muffled voice that's sometimes hard to understand. And that led to a crazy misunderstanding right off. He was looking down at my records and said something that sounded like, "How long is your prick?"

I was a little surprised, but when you've seen as many doctors as I have, you're ready for anything.

"About seven and a half inches," I said.

He looked up as if I were crazy and asked again, but much slower and louder, "How long was your trip?"

I really felt pretty stupid as I tried to explain, "I thought you asked how long was my prick."

"Our studies have shown that that information is not very important," he said, and smiled very slightly. At least it broke the ice.

I found out two things about Dr. Masters pretty quickly. First, he refused to accept vague descriptions about sexual things. No generalities. And second, as I watched his face, I realized nothing I'd ever done would shock him.

For instance, during that first session we got into masturbation. That's a subject I'd talked about often enough with analysts, and all I ever said usually was, "I did it a lot as a kid," or "I was scared my parents would catch me." But that didn't do with Dr. Masters. I felt he wanted to know what hand I used, what kind of strokes I did, what I called it (Jerking off? Jacking off? Playing with yourself? Abusing yourself? What?), what my thoughts were when I did it. I told him how long it took me to come, whether I tried to come quickly or held back, how I felt about the amount of sperm I produced, how far it shot, whether I liked sperm or was disgusted by it.

The thing is, he didn't ask all these questions directly, but I sort of got the idea, and pretty soon I found myself talking like that. How sperm felt in my hand, how it smelled, how I hated the way it stiffened the sheets or stuck to the hairs of my legs in the bathtub. I thought about other people masturbating—my father, my wife, my mother. In ten minutes I talked more about masturbation than I had in all the rest of my life. It didn't seem dirty. It became something very interesting, almost fascinating. And by the way, I've enjoyed it much more ever since.

Another subject that came up, though, was different: Sex

with my first wife. Myra had an uncurable disease for five years before she died, and in that time her body became awful to me. I tried to explain how I felt about touching a deteriorating body and how I imagined that the motion of my penis inside her might be harming her and things like that. Then I found myself telling him about the awful night when we were having intercourse and Myra lost control of her bowels. It was terrible. Terrible. Yet here I was telling Dr. Masters about it the first hour I ever spent with him. When I finished I looked up and saw on his face the kindest expression I had ever seen on a human being. I sensed this man really understood about Myra.

Her nickname was "Legs" which is so sad to think about because when she became sick those lovely legs were the first part of her to go.

When I was seventeen, Myra did an incredibly thrilling thing. She walked up to me, touched me on the arm, and said, "I like you." She was so nervous and serious that she must have been thinking about it for months. It hit me like a bomb.

In five minutes we were having a Coke together. It was the first time I'd been alone with a girl.

A year later we were going steady.

Two years later we were married.

And twenty years later, thanks to Myra, I was a patient at Masters and Johnson.

I say "thanks to Myra," not because I'm trying to blame the dead for my failures. It's just that you can't understand my sexual problems without understanding my first marriage.

Myra and I agreed on the sexual limits we would observe before-hand. We'd solemnly say it would "be nice" though certainly "not the be-all" if we "stayed virgins even with each other" until we got married. We felt if people could stand to wait and not go the limit there would be more "enjoyment" because they had "acted right." We *believed* all that, particularly the word "right." It wasn't fear of pregnancy that kept us pure. It wasn't our parents or the Jewish religion. It was just "right." It was "more right" for a girl than for a boy, but it was "really right" for both of us.

We were reluctant to try anything. After we'd been going steady for six months, I opened her blouse and went inside with my hand. The reaction was shocking. It was as if we'd broken a commandment. The moment I got home I wrote her a *letter:* "It was terrible of me. I'll never do it again. Forgive me. I lost control." Do you know that after she died she still had that letter among her things?

By the time of our wedding

    I had never seen her naked.
    She had never seen me naked.
    I had never touched her "there."
    She had never touched me "there."
    I had never had an orgasm in her company.
    She had never had an orgasm in my company.
    We had never even referred to any of our sexual parts by name.

But there was one thing Myra knew nothing about. Thanks to the United States Army I had finally gotten laid.

Less than a month after graduation from Fairfax I was in the army. I spent basic training at Camp Roberts, and the arrangement with Myra was that we'd be married after I finished basic.

I made two great buddies in camp. We were so close we even knew one another's serial numbers. "Hi there, 5678908," we'd say. Very corny, but what terrific pals we were. One of them, August L., I've lost sight of. But Charlie P. and I still keep in touch. He lives in Oxnard and I call him every Christmas.

One night Charlie had some news that made me dizzy.

"I met a girl tonight who is a nymphomaniac."

"How do you know?" (It was a struggle to keep calm.)

"I had her myself, and she said she'd take on as many guys as I could bring around. All at once. Separately. She doesn't care."

"She's probably a prostitute," I said.

"No, that's just it. She's rich. She's nice. She's simply a nympho. She *calls* herself a nymphomaniac. Actually used the word about herself."

Actually used the word. My God! I was so hot I was nearly sick.

I had been praying for a nymphomaniac since I was twelve years old. "Please God, just one, just once." They had become like holy beings to me. The mere definition could drive me wild. "Nymphomania"—morbid and uncontrollable sexual desire in a female. Morbid! Uncontrollable! And Charlie P. had actually found one!

Her name was Norma and she was perfect. Polite. Well-dressed. Virtuous-looking. The kind of girl we used to call "clean cut."

What she gave me that day was an unforgettable sense of *freedom*. For once nothing had to be hidden or hinted at.

Was there a bulge in my pants? I could talk about it.

"Look what you've done to me," I said.

"Gee, look at that. I can't wait," she said.

I was free to ask her *anything*. "How many times a day do you like it? Where do you like it best? Have you ever tried it in the rear? Ever used a French tickler?"

Does it sound dirty? You're *wrong*. It wasn't until after Masters and Johnson that I was able to feel as clean and unashamed about sex as I did that day with Norma.

Two things stand out.

She had taken off all her clothes and was lying, legs spread apart, on the back seat of a car. "I love to *ask* for it," she said. "So may I *ask* you to put your penis inside of me?" It was actually touching.

And, most memorable of all, as I was coming inside her, she kept saying, "Thank you. Thank you. Thank you."

When I told Dr. Masters that part of the story and how it still made me feel sexy, he said, "Thank *you*, Norma, wherever you are."

I dropped Norma off afterward in a very expensive-looking section of LaJolla and drove directly to an army pro station to have my penis cleaned. I couldn't take a chance on VD because Myra and I were getting married in less than a week.

We were to spend the "first night" at the Beverly Wilshire Hotel and fly to San Francisco the next morning for our honeymoon.

On the way to the hotel, a series of "don't's" ran through my mind:

>Don't hurt her.
>Don't act embarrassed.
>Don't lose your erection.
>Don't come too fast.
>Don't worry about the blood.

I was also slightly worried that I'd picked up an undetected case of VD from Norma. I'd heard of girls becoming pregnant the first time, but getting syphilis? God! I decided that if I passed it on to Myra, I'd kill myself.

The undressing went well. "I've always been so embarrassed by my breasts in gym class," Myra said, "but here I'm not."

We begin. Calmly. Solemnly. Then her fingernails dig into my back.

"I'm sorry," she says, "it hurts."

My erection vanishes. "Want to wait a little while?" I ask, and the words "unconsummated marriage" cross my mind.

"No, let's try."

And so silently, praying I'll remain hard enough to break her hymen, I try again. Her fingernails go deeper into my back. I know she's trying not to cry out. Then, a slight moan and her hands slowly relax.

We've done it. Later I see her blood. I think of my foot breaking the wineglass after the rabbi pronounced us man and wife.

For three years we had what you'd call a happy marriage and a normal, if unadventurous, sex life.

Then, suddenly, the impossible happened.

She was always tripping. She'd trip getting out of the car. On the stairs. Walking down a movie aisle.

Our first diagnosis now seems so pathetically naïve that it's almost funny. Do you know what we decided she had? "Weak ankles." *Weak ankles!*

And our treatment? "Sensible shoes." But Myra was too proud of her legs for that. "I'd rather fall down once in a while," she said. So when she'd trip, we'd make Dr. Scholl jokes and forget about it. Nobody goes to a doctor for "weak ankles."

Then she began complaining about her eyesight. We went to an eye doctor, but he didn't think she needed glasses. One morning about a month later she said to me, "I see two of you."

"Rub your eyes," I said.

"I still see two of you."

We made another appointment with the eye doctor, and while he was examining her, she suddenly said, "I have a crazy idea. Do you think I trip a lot because of my eyes?" You've got to hand it to that doctor. He must have guessed the truth the moment she asked that question, because he insisted we see a neurologist at Cedars of Lebanon.

At Cedars we found out it wasn't weak ankles or bad eyes. Myra had a disease of the central nervous system.

It was incurable. Nobody even knew its cause. We were told that Myra could live many years with it. They called it "intermittent"—there would be good as well as bad periods. We were told that a "breakthrough" was always possible. In short, we were told to hope. And we did. From doctor to doctor to doctor. We never lost hope. They weren't quacks. It's simply that they had nothing to give us *but* hope.

For seven years I watched her degenerate. Her speech became slurred, and as she talked, her head would nod violently. She developed a lurching walk, then tremors in her arms and legs. Her bladder became unpredictable. Then the symptoms would suddenly vanish, sometimes for long periods. Once they disappeared so completely we decided to have a child, although we were warned not to. Barbara was born and everything still remained okay. But in Barbara's infancy, the symptoms began to return. Still, Myra managed to care for the child until she was almost three years old. It was, I think, the most gratifying period of her life.

However, the good periods become shorter and the bad periods longer, and the symptoms grow more unpleasant. Eventually, Myra was bedridden.

Hard as it may be to believe, we managed to have a sex life of sorts during most of her illness. In the first stages it was still possible for me to enter her, but as she began to have less and less sensation below the waist, I felt as though I was using her as a receptacle. I also felt that I might be bruising her, though the doctors told me this was impossible. Then a queer thing happened. Her legs almost useless, she became more sensitive in her breasts, her mouth, and her hands. It was as if her sexual center of gravity had shifted. She'd want me to place my penis between her breasts so she could give me orgasms that way. I know she enjoyed it, too. During some of the "good periods" she began showing an interest in oral sex. And occasionally we'd still try to have intercourse.

Then because she was bedridden the bedsores began. They became so serious that I could barely bring myself to look at the lower part of her body. As they grew worse, I found it difficult to have any sexual contact with Myra. No matter what we did I would think of the sores. It was then that I first found myself losing erections. Even in masturbation I'd have difficulty staying erect. No matter what my fantasy, the sores would intervene.

The bedsores actually killed Myra, not the disease. One of them worked its way so deeply inside her that it became embedded in the joint of her hip and became infected. The poison spread throughout her body and she fell into a coma. I stayed in the hospital for ten days waiting for her to come out of that coma, and she did and we were able to take her home. But two months later, it happened again and this time she developed pneumonia. I was with her at the end and saw the last shudder.

Some people believe everything in life must have a point. I'd like to tell you two things that Myra said in the last week of her life. One night she said, "I'm only twenty-six, but I've had love and a family and a home, so if I die I can't say I haven't been alive." And the very next afternoon she said, "What's so horrible is that I have not lived at all."

JOAN

Monday Afternoon

St. Louis was freezing after Los Angeles, so while I took a nap Monday afternoon in our hotel room, Harold did a very sweet thing. He went out and rented a car. He said it would turn out in the long run to be cheaper than taxis, and anyhow he didn't want me standing around in the cold when taxis were hard to find.

Late that afternoon we took a drive around the city and then went to a nice restaurant called Nantucket Cove. I began to relax. What had started out so tensely the night before was calming down a little.

JOAN

Tuesday Morning

When we arrived at the clinic, I was impressed by everyone's friendliness and the way they remembered who we were. I mean, there was obviously a very steady flow of patients—Harold and I had been lucky to squeeze our two weeks in so quickly—yet the receptionists and secretaries took time to say nice things about what I was wearing, and they all remembered our names.

Dr. Masters, as Harold told me, was completely professional and not as warm or friendly as Mrs. Johnson. He said, "Good morning, good morning," very briskly as I came in and he sat me down right away. When he talked he held a letter opener by its ends with the tips of his two forefingers, and occasionally used it to point or emphasize something.

He surprised me, and yet helped put me at my ease, by talking at first about himself. He said he began his professional life as a gynecologist, and then discovered how few people, including doctors, knew anything about sex. He decided to look into it seriously. He went back to school and studied psychiatry, and for eighteen months practically lived with a group of prostitutes to find out all he could about male and female reactions to sex. The prostitutes were the only ones at the time who would talk openly about sex with him, but of course he paid them for it. Later, when he got Virginia Johnson to help him with his work, there were years of laboratory research. They studied the inside of a woman's vagina, for instance, with a plastic penis which had a tiny built-in camera and lights, and discovered that the vagina secretes a cream which allows a man to enter, and that it swells in heat and open like a flower as a man's penis comes in.

Dr. Masters and his stories were fascinating. He wasn't handsome, yet he was somehow attractive because of his masculine, virile ways. His manner was forceful, and you tended to do what he said. Then he suddenly stopped talking about himself and pointed the letter opener at me.

"How did you happen to come here?" he asked. "Was it your idea or your husband's? Did both of you come willingly?"

I told him just how it happened. He nodded.

"Now what's your story?"

He wanted to know about Harold and me from the beginning, so I started from the time we first met when Norman G. introduced us. I didn't leave anything out because I felt I shouldn't be the one to decide what was important and what wasn't.

One of my friends, when I worked at the movie studio, was a fellow in the set department named Norman G. One day, Norman called me up and said he knew this Jewish fellow in the furniture business, square but nice, a solid family type who might be a good change for me. I'd had enough swingers and wiseguys for a lifetime, he said. Of course he was right about that, but this Harold K. he brought around sure was a sad case. I mean he had everything going against him—a wife who'd just died and a penis that seemed dead, too, although I had no doubt I could bring that to life. I felt sorry for the guy, sure, but what did I want with a loser?

And then, I don't know, somehow he started to get to me. He wasn't a swinger, that's for sure, and he wasn't the most cultured guy in the world, but you could see he had possibilities. He was good looking without being pretty, physically strong from wrestling furniture, considerate and generous, easy to be with. But what mattered more was that he wasn't a nut who would float away to sea or shack up somewhere with a boy. I could tell about people. This was a solid citizen from a real family, a responsible adult who'd be around tomorrow and next week and maybe for the rest of my life. That was a pretty big thing for a girl who'd had so many one-night stands.

And I saw right away that he loved me. He didn't just come around for sex, he liked to talk to me, and I felt sorry for him, so I did what I could to help. I went to bed with him, and although it didn't work out, I figured it was tied in with his wife problem.

One night he and his brother and sister-in-law and I had dinner out together. Afterward, when they were driving me home, Harold and I were smooching a little in the back seat. He put his arms around me and gave me a kiss good night... and it was like in the books. The earth of Los Feliz Drive turned, birds in eucalyptus trees made music, and I didn't want Harold to leave. Twenty minutes later he called on the phone and, after talking for two or three hours, agreed we were in love.

He let his stepmother-in-law take his daughter into her house, and he moved in with me. The girl was about twelve then and a pretty mixed-up kid. Her mother had been so sick and unable to take care of her for three or four years, and Harold wasn't much of a father because of all his troubles. I felt I could help the situation, and I really thought I loved Harold enough to marry him. I wasn't too worried about the sex thing because I figured that was just a carry-over from the first wife and would straighten out sooner or later.

But living together turned out to be pretty rocky, and there was no prospect of Barbara's being able to move in with us. We were having too much trouble ourselves. We had some rare success with sex but not very often, and sometimes we had some bad fights because I was hung up at not getting the normal sex I wanted or because I felt frustrated that I couldn't get him aroused properly. The fights would usually end with Harold packing his bag and marching out of the place. He came and went so often my neighbors were never sure which way he was headed when they saw him with a bag.

As a matter of fact, he marched out one night after we'd had one of our battles, and two minutes later he marched right back in. He picked me up from the sofa where I was watching TV and said, "You want to get married?"

I said, "Sure."

"When?"

"How about now?"

"Now?" That stopped him for a minute, but only for a minute. "OK, now. Go inside and get dressed."

Norman came along as our witness. We drove all night and got married in Las Vegas in the morning and then had a champagne breakfast. We got back to LA the next day and Harold realized it was Mother's Day, and he suddenly was filled with guilts. He dropped me at my apartment and went off to see his mother without me. I went upstairs and cried, but he called me from her house and apologized and came back as quickly as he could. I suppose if he wasn't thoughtful about his mother, he couldn't be the person I loved. And in some ways I'm just as old-fashioned as he is, like about faithfulness.

Dr. Masters hadn't said a word during all this, just nodded his head now and then and rocked a little in his chair. Now he leaned forward and rested one hand on his desk.

"Your sex life since then has been pretty thin outside of masturbation, hasn't it?" he asked.

I nodded and hesitated for a moment, wondering whether or not I should tell him about Dunbar. Then I realized I had to.

"There *was* one thing," I said, "which I'm going to tell you about. I told it yesterday to Mrs. Johnson and I'm going to ask you what I asked her: Please don't tell Harold."

"I won't if you ask me not to."

"The thing is, I think it would kill him."

Dr. Masters just looked at me. I didn't know what he meant by his silence.

"Do you think I'm wrong about that?" I asked.

"I think it would be wrong for me to give any opinion," he said. "Suppose you just tell me the story."

So I told him the Dunbar story and then asked him again not to repeat it to Harold. He promised he wouldn't.

HAROLD

Tuesday Morning

I had never been treated by a lady therapist and imagined I might feel a little embarrassed with Mrs. Johnson. Instead, I felt aroused. She's very sexy.

It's not so much what she looks like, it's what she's seen.

Whenever I come across a picture of Jackie Kennedy I think, *Those are the eyes that saw what happened in Dallas.* It's as if a person's experience shows.

Well, Mrs. Johnson has seen more sex than any other woman in history. She's watched it, timed it, measured it, weighed it, taken its temperature, felt its pulse, analyzed its juices, heard its noise. She's thought about it all day, every day, for thirteen years. And when I met her, I couldn't think of anything else.

Instead of talking about my problems, do you know what I really wanted to say to her? "Tell me some stories."

Mrs. Johnson, who had been trained in psychology and sociology, joined Dr. Masters as a research assistant in 1957. The idea of the "Dual Sex Therapy" team came out of their association. At Masters and Johnson every couple is treated by two therapists, one male and one female.

Having a therapist of your own sex means you've got someone who intuitively understands things you may not have the words for. "It takes one to know one," Dr. Masters says.

Two therapists also reduce the possibility of getting biased information. If you tell a story one way to Dr. Masters and another way to Mrs. Johnson, they can cross-check, so you tend not to show off or lie in the first place.

On Monday I imagined Mrs. Johnson had learned how Joan felt about me. I supposed she now wanted to know my thoughts about Joan.

She casually mentioned how "at home" she felt with Joan. That instantly sent me into my usual routine of, "Yes, isn't Joan a marvelously warm, bright, fascinating girl who etc. etc."

I told her how "lucky" I was to have found her and how Joan must have "walked under a ladder" the day she met me.

Mrs. Johnson hadn't asked a single question, but I think she'd taken me right where she wanted me to be.

I told her what a "nut" I thought Joan was when I first met her and how I couldn't imagine why she kept seeing "a slob like me."

The first words Joan ever said to me were, "You look miserable."

Actually, I don't mind a quick insult from a girl. It shows

interest. And it was obvious that she *was* interested. Before I'd got past her door I think she spoke 10,000 words. "Relax, relax . . . I don't bite . . . how did you get so pale in California . . . I like your sports coat . . . Norman said your wife died . . . How do you like my furniture . . . you're in furniture, aren't you . . . don't look so unhappy . . . sit down . . ."

Next she was speeding around the room making drinks, finding cigarettes, punching pillows, shifting chairs, turning on lamps, looking in mirrors, searching for matches. I'd met The Human Tornado! Norman G. had given me her number. "She's easy to be with," he said, "I also hear she loves to fuck. Or was it suck?"

We drove to the Santa Ynez Inn where she barely touched her food because she was telling me her life story. And when we got back to her apartment, she invited me up because, "I haven't told you anything yet." You know, I loved all those words! She really made me feel alive.

But the moment we got inside the apartment I felt scared. I thought that to be "manly" I should probably make a pass at her. But I'd learned with Myra that I couldn't trust my penis.

So instead I told her the same story I'd been telling prostitutes. Confession was easier than embarrassment I'd discovered.

It really quieted her.

"You mean *nothing* will make that thing of yours stand up," she said when I was through.

"Nothing," I said with a shrug.

Long pause. I could see the story had struck some kind of chord. She seemed to be thinking very hard.

"Let me try something," she said. And without another word, she undid my pants, and very carefully took out my penis and placed it in the wettest, warmest mouth I'd ever felt in my life. I didn't get an erection, but I came.

HAROLD: *Tuesday Morning* 57

"You came *soft!*" She was absolutely stunned. I've never felt anything so exciting in my life. "Imagine, you came *soft!*"

I think she got so excited because she thought she'd caused a great breakthrough in my sex life. I guess I'd neglected to tell her that I practically *always* came soft.

But a different sort of breakthrough *had* occurred. For months I'd wanted to go down on a girl, but I hadn't met the proper one. I didn't dare try it with prostitutes, since I was too afraid of VD. And the one "nice girl" I dated since Myra's death hadn't aroused me that way. But Joan was definitely the proper one. And did she go crazy that first night, screaming, kicking, pummeling my head and pulling my hair!

For the first time in years I had actually given sexual pleasure to another person.

We began seeing each other after that. I think I must have been some kind of project for her. I felt she was *nursing* me sexually (Virginia Johnson winced when I used that word). And we'd have little successes now and then. Even intercourse. *But never two days in a row.* If I'd get an erection on Monday, Tuesday was guaranteed to be a washout. Something, and it wasn't physical exhaustion, prevented me from putting two good days together.

Joan made sure I was never embarrassed by my failures. We'd invented an excuse we could both believe. "You're still not over your experiences with Myra." We knew, just knew, that time would take care of everything. Another hopeful sign: no matter how dismally I performed, Joan always seemed to be able to come.

She also began educating me. My lack of culture horrified her. She'd play snatches of classical records and ask me to identify the pieces. For a while she made me pledge to memorize a poem a week.

My friends, of course, were floored. They still are. Joan was prettier than anyone we knew. She dressed better and talked smarter. She was funny, interesting, and sexy. They'd say things to me like, "What have you been hiding in your slacks?" "What she sees in you I'll never know." It felt terrific!

The only people opposed to Joan were my parents who felt I was throwing my life away on a *shiksa*. Funny. I felt it was Joan who was throwing herself away on me. What was I? A furniture man with no education, no conversation, no sophistication. I couldn't even keep a hard-on.

We were married in Las Vegas. It took eighteen months before my parents would talk to her. Now they love her as much as I do.

Mrs. Johnson wanted to know how Joan was sexually when I first met her. "Oh, *quite* normal. She'd been around a lot and said she always had orgasms. No hang-ups at all."

"And now?"

"I'm sure she'd still be OK if only I were normal."

I explained they mustn't *blame* Joan for me. That as far as I could see my troubles came straight from Myra.

I told her how Joan was "such a great help in the business. I'm the money man, but she's the one with taste."

I mentioned how proud I felt when my friends came to the house.

"I think they're all hot for her," I said.

"Does that worry you?" she asked.

"Not with my friends, but a few years ago when she was still working, I thought about it once in a while."

"Does she worry about you that way?"

"Me? Impotent me!" I laughed. Mrs. Johnson didn't even smile. Then I said, "Once since our marriage I went to a prostitute." I made her swear not to tell Joan.

"Do you think telling her would make a difference?" she asked.

"I'm not sure," I said. "But why take a chance."

What did I mean "a chance"?

"It might hurt her," I said. "You know women."

"Only slightly better than I know men," Mrs. Johnson said.

I related a homosexual experience I'd forgotten to mention to Dr. Masters. I told her there was one detail I might find hard to tell a woman.

"When I was about ten, I think I was raped in the rear end by the janitor of our building. It's all completely vague to me except for one thing. Afterward, I remember feeling moisture coming out of my behind. I reached back and came up with what could only have been a handful of the janitor's sperm."

"Do you think it had any effect on you?" She had taken the story without blinking.

"I still feel a little queasy about wetness in sex," I said. "I don't like sweat or other moistures. Luckily Joan is a fanatic about cleanliness." We were back on Joan again. And for five minutes I went on about how much I admired her clean habits.

The meeting with Mrs. Johnson had been much easier than the one with Dr. Masters. To me it didn't seem nearly as dramatic. When I left, I felt I hadn't revealed as much to her as I had to him. Now that I think back, I may actually have told her more.

JOAN

Tuesday Afternoon

St. Louis turned out to be more of a place than we realized. Not fantastic, but nice. As we left the clinic on Tuesday, someone at the desk suggested we take the elevator ride to the top of The Arch, and the view was really spectacular. It was such a clear, sunny day, you felt you could almost see LA. The whole city of St. Louis was spread out below us, including a dirty brown river which, to my surprise, turned out to be the Mississippi. I'd learned about the Mississippi in grade-school geography class and still remembered one fact I'd never had a chance to use before. I said very casually to Harold, "It's two thousand, three hundred and thirty-one miles long, you know."

He looked at me in amazement, then finally said, "You don't say," and we both laughed. After that, whenever we saw a building or a statue, he asked me to tell him what it was, as though I was really an expert. We had fun.

We also enjoyed the Missouri Botanical Gardens because we're big plant people in our own backyard at home, and then we had a delicious Mexican dinner at a place called La Sala where we had champagne cocktails and tequila to wash down the frijoles and tamales and we giggled a lot.

Afterward we went to see *Bob and Carol and Ted and Alice,* a movie about two couples and their sex problems. The audience in the theater laughed a lot more than we did. But we were sort of amused at seeing this type of picture under the circumstances.

Then we went back to the hotel and bed. It was a nice day.

JOAN

Wednesday

  We got up early to be at the clinic at eight thirty for our physical check-ups. They sent us upstairs first to give blood samples, and the technician showed us their lab which was equipped to run every possible test on blood known.
 Then each of us was examined by a rather pretty female doctor who I'm sure wasn't thirty years old. She was very thorough, though. Harold said later she even made an anal check of his prostate gland. It occurs to me now that a man who didn't have my husband's problem might have been embarrassed at having such an attractive girl do an examination like that—you know, got an erection. Doctors aren't completely impersonal. I know I've been aroused by some of that pushing and probing they do. I wonder if that pretty girl was used on Harold purposely to see if he would have any reaction?
 I went into the session with Masters and Johnson a little nervously because of the Dunbar business, and half sorry I'd brought the damn thing up at all. I wasn't the sick one, Harold was. Why take a chance on trouble? If they told him about that, things would only be worse. But it was too late to do anything about it, so I just sat down and waited to see

what would happen. These two people had gotten more information out of us in a shorter time than anyone else before them. What would they do with it?

Dr. Masters began with a review of all the important points Harold and I had told them, especially the parts about friction between us; he seemed to think those really mattered. His review showed pretty clearly what we were to each other, but he felt a lot more would come. "The history of a relationship," he said, "is an unfolding story, and we expect further revelations and insights as we go along. Truly knowing each other is important."

He turned to Harold. "Now let's talk about you. You have what we call 'secondary impotence.' 'Primary impotence' is a condition describing a man who has never had an erection. In our opinion your impotence was induced, almost without question, by the trauma of that very unfortunate experience with your first wife."

You could almost hear the breath come out of Harold's mouth, and you could practically feel his sense of relief. He had always opposed the analyst's theories that his troubles came from his mother or his father or both, because he couldn't stand hearing criticism of them. He always argued that if they *were* responsible then why wasn't he impotent before that night with Myra? How come, he asked, he'd had no trouble with erections up to then?

So when Dr. Masters added that "This, quite simply and understandably, turned you off sex," Harold looked so grateful I thought he was going to stand up and shake the doctor's hand. He didn't, of course. He only nodded his head and shifted around in his seat and made a sound like a grunt. But I knew that Dr. Masters could ask him to walk on water right then and he'd try.

"We have a theory I'd like to tell you about," Dr. Masters said, still looking at Harold. "It's this: When a person in your condition tries to have sex there's always a third person in the room distracting you and taking your mind off what's happening. You feel you're being watched to see if you'll fail again. Sometimes the watcher is your first wife, sometimes it's your father, or a friend, or maybe a teacher from school. But most often that third person is you." He hesitated. "Or does that seem too farfetched to you?"

"No, no," Harold said quickly, "it isn't farfetched at all. I think I know what you mean."

"Good. The first thing we're going to do then is get rid of that third person, OK?" He nodded his head and didn't wait for an answer. "We're going to put you back to where you were originally. Better, as a matter of fact. You're going to learn things about sex I don't think you ever knew."

Harold was beaming now, you'd think he was cured already. Dr. Masters had a way of saying things with such confidence that you began to think they were true. But he also made lots of sense.

"Before we give you people instructions for your first lesson, let me explain a little bit more about this theory. That third person of yours makes it practically impossible for sex to function naturally for you. *Naturally*. The most important thing I can tell both of you—or anyone—is that sex is a normal, *natural* function. No healthy male, for example, has to be taught how to have an erection. If the stimuli are right it *has* to happen, just as surely as eating no food will make a person hungry and getting no sleep will tire him out. However, if a person is distracted enough, sex cannot and will not work, not properly. And again, it's like eating or sleeping. When you're upset it's quite possible to lose your appetite or have insomnia, isn't it?"

Harold nodded and said, "Of course."

"Well, Harold's a healthy man," I said, "I'm sure your report will show that."

"I hope so. In that case, I'm certain we'll be able to help him." Dr. Masters suddenly pointed the letter opener at me. "Now there's something I want to say to you."

The tone of his voice frightened me. *My God,* I prayed, *please don't let him talk about Dunbar.* He didn't.

"You think you know a lot about sex. Well, I'm asking you right now to forget all you think you know and start from scratch with your husband. We're going to try to fix things for both of you, which is why we have you both here. And that's one way, incidentally, in which we differ from psychiatrists. They treat individuals. We treat relationships. To us the relationship is the patient. So we're going to treat you, your husband, and the relationship—three for the price of one."

It was the closest thing to a joke I'd heard out of him in the three days we'd been coming to the clinic, and somehow for the first time he seemed more human. I grinned and so did Harold, and I remember I sat forward in my seat and even thought about taking a pencil and pad from my purse to make notes on what he'd tell us about our first lesson. It wasn't necessary. The instructions were simple and clear. Mrs. Johnson, who hadn't spoken till then but just watched us, explained part of it.

"We've found," she said, "that people don't really know each other in the simplest, most basic way. I mean, for instance, as basic as what excites women."

Harold nodded his head and I said, "I've never yet met a man who really knew what excites women."

"Well," Dr. Masters said, "we won't be concerned with what excites women generally. We want your husband to find out what excites you. And we want you to find out about him. And the best way to do that is to start with what we call the sensate focus, the use of the sense of touch."

"I've always loved to touch," I said, "and so has my husband."

"So do most people," said Mrs. Johnson. "Touch is a beautiful way of expressing sex as well as warmth, love, tenderness, many different emotions. I think you'll be surprised at what you can learn about each other merely by touching."

I asked, "Is there any particular time and place that we're supposed to do it?"

"Not really," she said. "The aim of the exercise is discovery and pleasure. Therefore find a time when both of you are feeling fairly relaxed and, if possible, close to each other. Go to your room in the hotel and take off all your clothes."

"For how long a period is this to be?"

"Do it in two sessions of about an hour each. Mr. K., you touch your wife first for about half an hour, lightly, gently, all over her body except for her genitals or breasts. Neither of you is to touch any sexual parts during this exercise."

"And remember it's not a massage," Dr. Masters said, "but a discovery. Put your hand on top of your husband's, Mrs. K.," he said to me, "and guide it to areas you find pleasurable. Talk as little as possible. Try to tell him with your hands whether you want a lighter or stronger touch."

"Instead of using bare hands, though," Mrs. Johnson said, "we'd like you to use a cream or lotion. Normally I'd give you a jar of a preparation we've made up ourselves. But we're temporarily out of it; we're waiting for a shipment. But there are many commercial preparations that will do as well. Stop in the building pharmacy on your way out this morning and get some lotion. One brand people like is Keri, but you get any other brand that appeals to you. Just put some on your hands before you start the touching."

"Dry hands can feel rough against the skin," Doctor Masters said, "and the lotion prevents that." We both nodded to show we understood. "Now two last things. First, if you get pleasure from the touching, don't feel you have to return the pleasure immediately to your partner. You will get your turn when the other's time is up. And finally, the ban on sex continues."

When we left the building with several jars of Keri lotion in my purse, we stopped on the sidewalk out front. I asked Harold if he wanted to go right back to the hotel.

He said, "Let's walk a little," and that was all right with me. They said we shouldn't rush things, so I didn't mind playing it cool. I wondered if Harold was nervous in any way but decided not to ask him. I didn't want to put the idea in his head if it wasn't there to start with.

We took a pretty long walk, then went back for our car and drove to the hotel. Harold said he was hungry, but when we stopped at the coffee shop on the roof of our hotel neither of us ate very much. When we finally took the elevator downstairs to our room I think we were both slightly nervous.

The maid had already been in. Everything was neat and clean, there were fresh gold-colored sheets on the enormous bed which was an oversized double. Harold locked the door behind us and we stood and looked at each other.

"You excited?"

"Yes," I said. "You?"

He nodded. Without another word we both removed our clothes and then stood naked and looked at each other again.

"Should we kiss?"

"They said not to touch each other's sexual parts. If we hug, we're bound to t—"

"OK, sure," Harold said. He turned and got the jar of Keri lotion.

I lay down on the bed and Harold came over and looked at me. I suddenly thought maybe I'd made a mistake. Lying on my back and all. I mean, he might think it was a challenge, you know, to try sex in spite of what Dr. Masters had said. So I quickly turned over so he'd be looking at my back instead of my breasts and pubic area.

Harold climbed on the bed and straddled me, and for a moment his penis brushed across my back, but then he shifted his weight and leaned over to start applying the lotion. I smelled it as he put some on his hands and then set the jar back on the bed table. The scent excited me. I closed my eyes and waited for Harold to start.

Suddenly, more gently than ever before in his life, Harold put his hands on my back and smeared the cool, smooth lotion across it. Instantly I was aroused. I've never known anything so fast. I knew I was wet between my legs and my nipples were hard, and the feel of Harold's hands was unbelievable. He had always been rough with me, but now his touch was gentle. Maybe it was the lotion, or maybe he was really feeling me for the first time.

He stroked my shoulders and the back of my neck, down along my back and fleetingly over my backside. Then he shifted his position slightly and stroked the soles of my feet, and my toes and ankles and up along my legs and thighs. I suddenly started to moan. It must have been exciting for him, too, because he began whispering, "You're beautiful . . . You're so beautiful. . . ."

He covered all of my back from the neck down to the tips of my toes until I could feel my body jumping underneath his hands. In all of the ten years that we had been married, he had never had me like this before.

After he finished with my back I turned over. He desperately wanted to touch my breasts. Of course, I wanted him to touch them, too, but we knew we weren't allowed. Harold put more lotion on his hands and gently caressed my throat and then outwards to my shoulders and then down my entire body. It was fantastic. He didn't touch my breasts or any of the genital area, but in some ways I found it more exciting because it was so tantalizing. He came so close so often that several times I found my body pushing upward toward his hands. Occasionally I covered his hand with mine and guided it, the way Dr. Masters said, to things I especially liked. I started to moan again.

After about an hour or so—we'd forgotten to look at the clock—Harold lay down beside me. Without thinking about it I leaned over and kissed him on the lips and our mouths opened and our tongues touched. He put a hand on my shoulder and then let it start down to my breast, but suddenly both of us stiffened and we pulled away from each other. We didn't want to cheat. This was too important.

We rested a little while and then I got up and straddled him. I was anxious to make it as good for him as he had for me. Anyhow I've always loved my husband's body because he's beautifully built. But that day I discovered to my surprise that his back is full of muscles I'd never noticed before. They must have come from lifting the heavy furniture in the store, but wherever they came from I loved the feel of them as I stroked with the tips of my fingers.

It was strange to look and touch that way and find things in a body you thought you knew completely. Every once in a while as I caressed him Harold pulled his breath in sharply, and then as he let it out he'd say, "Ooohh, do that again . . ." so I felt I was doing all right. He had a look on his face that said he was up on the moon. I guess I had that same expression, too, because I've never enjoyed anything so much that was not specifically sex. Half of it was physical, the other half was seeing his pleasure.

I did it for almost an hour then sank down exhausted beside him. Both of our bodies were shiny and slippery from the lotion. We lay still beside each other with a relaxed, happy sense of fatigue and no sexual tension. Harold took my hand.

"Sleepy?"

I nodded but didn't say anything. He turned and took me in his arms. Our greasy bodies stuck together, but we hardly noticed. We were both asleep in seconds.

Several hours later we woke with a start because of an odd slurping noise that sounded like a wet rubber suction cup leaving the side of a smooth surface. It was our two greased bodies coming apart.

HAROLD

Wednesday

I remember saying to myself, "This is not your first wife's body with her bedsores and everything. This is a completely new body."

I guess it was the first time in my life that I saw beauty in all parts of a woman. I kept saying, "You're so beautiful . . . you're so beautiful . . ." over and over again. Before, she was really just another woman to me, but this time I saw her as perfect and tender and clean. And it was so exciting it almost put me in a trance.

Joan didn't say anything while I was stroking her, but she moaned in a way I'd never heard before. It sounded like it came from some beautiful, happy animal. After half an hour or so we switched and Joan began stroking me.

Now, Dr. Masters had made it clear that we were not to have sex during this session, that we weren't even allowed to touch each other's sexual parts. But as Joan stroked me, I began to get a slight erection. And then, sure as hell, the minute I started getting hard, all the old fears began coming back. There I was feeling so good and I *still* couldn't get and hold an erection.

But it didn't feel quite as bad as usual. Dr. Masters had said, "Give it a chance. We can't cure it overnight."

HAROLD

Thursday Morning

The next morning we hurried out of bed and barely touched breakfast. We couldn't wait to get back to the clinic.

Maybe it's part of the treatment, but from the moment you arrive in St. Louis, Masters and Johnson keep you in a state of suspense. Each morning my first thought was, *"Now what?"* I don't really think they try to mystify their patients. Maybe each case is treated so differently, even Masters and Johnson aren't exactly sure "what's next." Anyhow, it doesn't make you nervous. Just keeps you interested.

We arrived before nine. The receptionist was just taking off her coat, but both Dr. Masters and Mrs. Johnson were already there. Is it possible they work twenty-four hours a day?

Dr. Masters gave us an especially cheery "Good morning," and eagerly asked, "How did it go?" He was grinning, Mrs. Johnson was grinning, we were grinning. Everyone *knew* it had gone well.

Congratulations all around.

Then Dr. Masters abruptly said "OK, back to business, tell me what you did *exactly*." Joan led off. She really gushed. First she described her own reactions in detail. And then she proceeded to describe mine. When she finished, Dr. Masters turned to me with a slight smile. "Have *you* anything to add?"

"I can't think of anything else," was all I said. That's how it was in those days. She was a pretty tough act to follow.

"Very good!" he said to both of us. Then, still all business, he began our next lesson.

"Some time today, I want you to go back home [he never called it the hotel, always "home"] and rub each other with the cream again. But now, *you* may touch her breasts, vagina, and clitoris, and *you* may touch his penis and testicles." He paused to let that sink in. "Just *touch*, I said."

"Here's how I want it done. It can only be done this way."

I was to lie with my back against the headboard and my legs spread. Joan was to sit between my legs, cradled in my arms, her back to my chest, her head resting on my shoulder.

"I want you to caress her face, eyes, cheekbones. I want you to *understand* her with your hands."

As he spoke, Dr. Masters moved his hands as if he were caressing an imaginary body.

"I want you to learn the textures of her breasts, nipples, vagina, and clitoris." He paused. "You know where they *are*, don't you?" I understand he sometimes gives a lecture at this point to couples who aren't completely familiar with each other's sexual parts. He had, however, already satisfied himself that Joan and I knew genitals pretty well. "I've met men who've been married for over twenty years and have never even heard of the clitoris," he had told us.

After I had caressed Joan for half an hour, we were to move into a different position. Joan was to be against the headboard and I was to lie between her outspread legs, facing her, with my head at the foot of the bed on a pillow, my genitals right on her lap.

She was to massage my penis with the lotion.

"Look at her face while she's stroking you. You may see her breasts swell and her face redden. It means she likes it."

Joan evidently was becoming very aroused. When he mentioned "breast swelling," she said, "Do you know what you're *doing* to me." It was no joke.

"Save it for later," Dr. Masters said, "right now I want you to listen to a very important thing."

He began describing what he called "sexual signals" . . . a way of telling each other what stimulates you.

"When Mrs. K. is stroking your penis, put your hand on top of hers and guide it to the part of your penis you want touched. If you want her to fondle you with a lighter or firmer touch, tell her with pressure from your hand."

He told Joan to do the same when I was stroking her.

He stressed touch signals but said, "You can also moan, groan, or even talk but *somehow* let each other know what you want."

The idea of sexual signals is one of the greatest things we learned in St. Louis. So few people realize they're entitled to *ask* for what they want in sex. Maybe they think it's dirty or unnatural to make a sexual request, but we found out that sex signals completely open up the world of pleasure.

Dr. Masters told us to use sexual signals as a part of the exercise. Later we realized they should be used in every form of sex. If your husband isn't touching your clitoris or your vagina the way you really like, put your hand on top of his and show him how to do it. You've been masturbating all your life, but how is he to know the touch you prefer?

If your wife doesn't know how to handle your penis, put your hand on hers and show her.

If you feel like oral sex, take her head in your hands and lead it toward your genitals. Why be subtle? What's more exciting than a direct request for a specific sex act?

To improve someone's sucking technique you don't have

to say "slower" or "faster" or "softer" or "deeper." It's more exciting to indicate what you want by the pressure of your hands. It works better too. (Joan must always have known this. When I was first going with her, I guess I wasn't sucking her nipples the way she really liked it done. So one day, she started to suck on my nipples. I was pretty surprised, since no one had ever done that to me before. When she was through, she said, "Now *you* do me *that* way." I knew just what she meant, something I could never have understood with words.)

"I'll let the two of you go now," Dr. Masters said. He must have realized we were pretty anxious to get back to the room. "But remember, no sex, no intercourse, just touching. We'll see you tomorrow at the same time."

JOAN

Thursday Afternoon

  On Wednesday Harold and I had played it cool after the session at the clinic with Masters and Johnson and took a long walk and a bite of lunch before going back to our rooms. On Thursday we didn't dawdle.

  As soon as we reached the hotel we parked the car and went right up to our rooms, not stopping this time for any lunch nonsense. The minute we entered the room we behaved like characters in a speeded-up movie. Pants and shorts and bra and shoes went flying like autumn leaves in a windstorm. We were naked so fast that both of us started to giggle, and as each of us leaped into bed we grabbed some Keri lotion.

  After a minute or so we got control of ourselves and turned to the serious business of carrying out our instructions. There was a little confusion at first about the positions we were supposed to take, but I finally convinced Harold that we were to start with him sitting up against the headboard, while I sat directly in front of him between his opened legs with my back to his chest and my head resting on his shoulder. He put his arms around me, but the position seemed slightly awkward so I turned slightly to my right until Harold and

I could look at each other comfortably. He was able to reach most parts of my body, certainly the ones we both wanted him to reach that day.

I guess I should point out quite frankly that Harold is a breast man. I mean, he really loves breasts. But on that Thursday afternoon in St. Louis, after hours the previous day of sensual caressing without touching sexual areas, I wanted his hands on my breasts just as much as he wanted to get at them. I couldn't wait for his touch. I didn't have to. That's where he went first.

It was beautiful. Not just because of the build-up the day before, it was beautiful for itself. That slippery, sexy lotion, for instance, had me excited practically before we started. And then there was that position. I'd never been fondled or caressed like that, and I found it very erotic. In addition, Harold had learned his lesson well the day before. He continued to be gentle and loving and soft and slow and he remembered the places I liked. But best of all, I must say, was the feel of his hands on my bosom. Again and again he went around and across, between and below my breasts till I was out of my mind. We just couldn't get enough.

Every once in a while I remembered what Dr. Masters had said about having Harold touch me everywhere, so I guided his hands away from my breasts, slick with the Keri lotion, to my face and neck and shoulders and stomach and then to the genital region. He ran a finger softly along my vagina and then moved up gently to my clitoris and then to the muscle above it. I was boiling over, almost out of control, but I certainly didn't stop him. I felt like one large vagina.

At the end of thirty minutes—we watched the clock this time—we rested a little while. We had done too much the previous day, so from now on we wanted to stick religiously to the instructions. We agreed it shouldn't be hard. After all, this treatment was a lot nicer than the medicines or diets some doctors prescribe, and although we had no visible results yet, we didn't mind being patient and obedient under these pleasant circumstances.

We switched positions, and again got a little confused about how to lie down so that Harold could watch my face and breasts and I could hold his penis. We finally figured it out. I put Keri lotion on my hands, cupped Harold's genitals in them for a moment, then gently began massaging. Now and then I ran a finger as sensuously as possible along the underside of his penis and the area down at the base. This made Harold moan and it aroused me somewhat, too, though that didn't take much doing. Between the long session the day before and the half hour of caressing I'd just gone through in that exciting new position, I was like California underbrush when there's been no rainy season: one spark and I was gone.

I looked at Harold and saw him staring at my face and breasts with wonder, awe, pleasure, surprise, and delight. I could guess what he was seeing. Dr. Masters had told him to watch me for signs of my excitement—a swelling of my breasts and a flush on my face, the marks of a woman in heat. Well, Harold saw I was aroused. There was no question about that.

And then, startling us both, Harold had an erection. It rose up right through my hands, surprising me because I honestly couldn't remember when it had happened last. It seemed to fill the room. Seven or eight glorious inches, maybe more. I couldn't know for sure. It seemed enormous to me and I guess to Harold, too. His eyes were very wide and his mouth hung partly open. It was probably twelve years since he'd had something like that, and I suppose he started thinking about it, because slowly it started to fade. But at least it had its moment, the first in years and years.

To people without our problem, what happened probably seems ridiculous and hardly worth discussing. But Harold's

JOAN: *Thursday Afternoon*

erections in the past had almost never come as a result of sex play, and those he did have were at best only semihard. So, too, were the ones he used to have at home which would cause him to grab for me wherever I was, even making dinner in the kitchen, and try to get it in me right then and there. That was romance for us.

Later that day, driving back to the hotel after dinner, I asked him whether he'd been conscious of the "third person" in the room when he had the erection.

"Not at first," he said. "I was busy watching your face and your breasts to see what would happen to them. That's all I could think about then. I was busy but I was enjoying myself, at least till I got the erection. Then other thoughts came in."

I didn't ask what they were. "I remember," I said, "that you closed your eyes just before it went down. I think maybe you should keep them open, keep on looking at me."

"Maybe," Harold said, his mind on something else. "Maybe."

HAROLD

Thursday Afternoon

I once read that perch and other fish are sexually active on sunny days, but if a small cloud temporarily covers the sun they stop making love until the cloud passes.

I think I know exactly what those fish go through. That's just they way my penis behaved that afternoon.

My erection was truly giant, if I say so myself. Have I mentioned that my penis is quite large? It has been measured at seven and a half to eight inches, fully erect. Even my semi hard-ons are about five and a half inches. This time it was definitely full length and very stiff. Just to see what would happen, I asked Joan to let go of it for a moment, and it stood up by itself, at a forty-five-degree angle. When I saw that thing pointing up instead of hanging down, it was really a proud moment. Oh, woodsman, spare that tree!

Joan kept stroking it, and for a while it seemed it might never go down.

Then came the first cloud.

It was Dr. Masters, smiling, saying "Good. Good for you!" We had a few brief words together and then my penis began to wilt.

I'd made the mistake of imagining myself sitting in Dr.

Masters' office the next morning telling him the good news. He himself had become "the Third Man."

I still think I could have got another, if it hadn't been for Joan. She still denies this, but when my penis began to wilt, I'd swear a look of contempt crossed her face. She kept on fondling it and the look lasted only a split second, but I had seen it, and that was cloud number two. After that, there was no chance of getting another.

Don't get me wrong, the session had been wonderful. I knew the erection was a definite step forward. And Joan's body felt even better to me than on the first day. Do you know what part I enjoyed most, by the way? Even sexier than her clitoris or her nipples, was stroking her cheekbones and her eyes.

But the most significant thing that happened in the session didn't occur to me until hours later, long after we'd bathed, dressed, and gone out for dinner.

We were in a restaurant and Joan made a remark about a woman who passed by our table. "What lovely legs she has," she said.

I instantly thought of Myra and suddenly realized that throughout the entire session Myra's body had not once crossed my mind. Maybe *that* cloud had passed for good.

When we got back to the room, the faint odor of the lotion was still in the air. Joan smelled it and gave me a little seductive smile. "Too bad we're not supposed to do it again," she said. The odor affected me that way too. I guess it had become like an aphrodisiac to us. I told her I wanted to do it as much as she did, "But let's try to stick to the rules."

When we got into bed, sex was so much on our minds we were afraid to kiss each other good night.

HAROLD

Friday Morning

This time Dr. Masters hadn't a chance for even one "Good morning." Joan was off and running before we sat down.

"We had one! We had one! We had one *like this.*" She spread her hands to indicate an erection about the size of a barracuda. Then she went into the details.

I said nothing. Just sat there thinking, "She tells it much better than I could."

And then an extremely important thing happened.

Dr. Masters glanced over at me as if to say, *"You* tell me. Did it *really* happen?"

I nodded at him.

A happy look came over his face. He gave me an understanding wink and turned back to Joan.

That was all. But that brief wordless communication said, "Dr. Masters is on *my* side." It felt terrific, as if I'd come out first in some kind of race. I wondered if Joan had noticed.

Until that glance, I was embarrassed about saying so little in these four-way sessions. I'd wondered "Does Dr. Masters think I'm stupid?" My silence in company has always made me squirm. But his glance had unquestionably said, "You don't talk too little. *She talks too much.*"

Believe it or not, I'd never dared think that before. I'd always admired Joan for being articulate, especially around people with advanced education. But now I found myself thinking, "Why doesn't she shut her big mouth?"

I heard her tell Dr. Masters ". . . then he lost it."

"Do you know *why* I lost it?" My first words of the session.

"Why?" asked Joan.

"Because of that *look* of yours."

"*What* look?"

"That look of contempt you gave me when I lost my erection."

"I did *not!*" Her glance at Dr. Masters indicated that I'd probably gone crazy.

"Honey, there was *some* kind of look on your face," I said.

"Honey, there *wasn't,* and if there was it was sympathy not contempt."

What a distinction! To a man failing sexually, what possible difference is there between contempt and sympathy. You'd almost *prefer* contempt.

Dr. Masters uttered his first words of the session, "Drop it. I'm glad it's out, but drop it."

Silence. I felt comfortable. Joan looked injured. I wondered what Mrs. Johnson was thinking.

"Good morning," said Dr. Masters finally. It cleared the air. He acted as if he hadn't witnessed our argument and began our next lesson.

"I want you to do the same thing as yesterday, using the same positions."

Joan looked disappointed. "That's *all?*"

"Didn't you like it yesterday?"

"Yes, but we thought there'd be something new."

"What's our hurry," he said. "We've got nothing but time."

Joan had another idea. "We did something *wrong* yesterday, didn't we?"

Dr. Masters was very patient. "Please don't think that. You were perfect yesterday. Both of you were fine. Really. It's just that we want you to do it again."

He turned to me. "And stop worrying whether you get an erection or not. *That's not the idea.* You're not supposed to have an erection. You're just supposed to enjoy touching and being touched."

You know, I believed him. For the first time having an erection didn't seem like a matter of life or death.

And then the session was over. Just before we left, he said, "Remember, no intercourse. No sex. Just touching. See you tomorrow."

It was 9:45; the session had taken less than fifteen minutes, by far the shortest meeting we'd had yet.

As we walked to the car I realized I'd forgotten to tell Dr. Masters that he'd appeared as "The Third Man." I made a mental note to tell him next time, but such an incredible thing was to happen before then that he never did find out. I'm sorry, because I'd like to know if it was something that happened to their other patients.

We were in no rush to return to the room. We decided to drive around Forest Park and look at the Greenhouses. Later Joan said, "It wasn't contempt, honey. Don't be mad." I wasn't in the least bit mad.

JOAN

Friday Afternoon

I was pretty eager to try again on Friday to see what would happen. It's true we hadn't exactly walked on water yet, but I considered Thursday's events a minor miracle and so did Harold.

In addition, though I hadn't thought about it much and certainly hadn't said anything, I was very proud of Harold and the way he'd been all week. Sure, I knew that Masters and Johnson said both of us were the patient, and I didn't disagree, of course. But still and all, no matter how you say it, the pressure was all on Harold. *He* was still the guy who had to deliver, *he* had to have the erection, a thing he'd been chasing so frantically all these terrible years. I knew the strain he was under, yet he never once whined or complained.

In the room we stripped off our clothes and assumed our positions again with me leaning against Harold's chest, both of us sitting up. I turned my head a little and kissed him on the cheek as he put his arms around me. I loved him a lot right then and prayed that what we were doing was not just another mistake.

The thirty minutes that followed were great, just like the day before. Maybe better. Being made love to that way was restful, exciting, relaxing, and mind-blowing. Harold was great.

When we switched and I massaged his genitals again, I saw him watching my breasts swell and I guess my face was flushed. Harold seemed mesmerized, entranced, whatever you want to say. And the miracle happened again. He had another erection, and this time it didn't go down almost as fast as it came up. This one seemed built to last, though I didn't stop to admire it. I made love to it with both slippery hands and Harold moaned and groaned.

I guess it lasted a minute, maybe two, but it was easily the longest erection, in size and duration, that Harold had had in almost thirteen years. I nearly burst with pride for him and wanted to kiss the pleased expression he had on his face. At the same time, I was very aroused myself.

We never had lunch that day. After the hour of lesson, we fell asleep in each other's arms. I woke up in the late afternoon to find Harold nibbling at my breasts with his lips. In seconds I was fully awake and thoroughly aroused. He held me tight. He had an erection, and he was as excited sexually as I've ever seen him. Our three days of sex play had really stirred his juices.

"Let me put it inside," he said, which of course didn't surprise me.

"No, Harold, we shouldn't." I wondered why the hell it was always the woman's job to say no. "You know we're not allowed to."

"I won't do anything really. I just want to put it in a little bit . . . just to see what it feels like."

He had that serious, earnest look on his face, like a little boy begging a favor. I groaned. How could I turn him down, especially when I was just as hung up as he was. All this foreplay was getting pretty heavy. I said, "All right, just a little bit."

JOAN: *Friday Afternoon*

We were lying on our sides and we didn't even try to get in the normal position, I mean with Harold mounting me, because we weren't having sex, we were just playing around a little. One of my legs was under the curve of his waist, so I put the other one up over his buttocks. We were facing each other on our sides, our slippery bodies still against each other.

He got his penis inside me easily because I was very wet down there, had been almost continuously, in fact, since almost the first lesson on Wednesday. And even though he didn't have an erection as big as the one in the morning it felt awfully good in there. He kissed me and held me tight and we felt very close to each other in more than a physical sense. We just lay still for a while enjoying each other's presence, not moving or speaking. Suddenly I had this incredible feeling. His penis was growing and swelling inside me, getting harder and longer, seeming to fill my vagina. I felt every part of it in me.

I was not just surprised, I was shocked and started to say so to Harold. But at that moment he completely went out of his mind—Harold exploded with the orgasm of his life, the first honest, normal release for him in who could remember when. He thrashed and howled and jerked madly for maybe ten seconds or so and then sank back exhausted.

"What was that?" I said to him, astonished and delighted.

"I don't know," Harold answered. He seemed stunned. "I can't understand it."

"You had an orgasm. **You** had a giant, colossal erection inside and then came like **Mount** Vesuvius. Pow!"

"Jesus, yes, I guess so." **Harold** grinned a little, half-pleased with himself and half-guilty about what happened.

I wondered what Dr. Masters was going to say about this. After all our careful vows, look what we'd gone and done.

The sheer surprise and unexpectedness of what happened to Harold had momentarily shocked me out of my own sexual excitement. Then guilt drove it away completely. At least for the time being. When it was time for bed that night, I put on one of the black, transparent, knee length nightgowns I'd purposely brought to St. Louis and Harold had a hard time keeping his hands off me. My tongue was soon hanging out again.

But I worried about whether we'd done anything to harm the progress of the treatment.

HAROLD

Friday Afternoon

That moment was worth the whole $2,500.

I wasn't a dead man after all. My penis was still in working order. There was hope.

It actually had *stayed* hard long enough for me to get inside her.

It *stayed* hard inside her. I could actually feel it growing stiffer and longer inside her. I felt I was filling her up with hardness.

And best of all, when I came—and it was such an exciting come that I wanted to shriek—when I came it was *still* hard. It became soft only after all my spasms were over and all my semen had drained.

What I've described is, I guess, just a normal everyday fuck. Well, a normal everyday fuck is what I've been trying to have for years. And "a fuck" is what you had to call it. It wasn't "sexual intercourse," or "love making" or "copulation." That day, I was fucking.

As I tell this story, it occurs to me that I haven't even mentioned Joan. Maybe that's part of it. My mind was only on one thing. I wasn't conscious of Joan or Myra or Masters or Johnson or even of myself. I was focused on that one part of me and the pleasure I was getting from the movements it made.

Afterward, Joan acted guilty because we'd gone against Dr. Masters' orders. I really didn't give a damn. All I knew was for the first time since I can remember I had made it.

We thought we'd found a solution once before. It was a sexual device that might have maimed me. But it *had* worked.

Impotent men are suckers for all kinds of "sexual accessories." We'll literally try anything that promises an erection.

You feel like a pervert the first time you send for one of these things. But after a while you turn it into sort of a scientific game. And if the ads are worded right, you can even feel like "a swinger."

Sexual devices aren't hard to find. If you are on the right mailing list, they'll find you. I must have made the lists about five years ago with my first purchase, a "miracle" product called, I believe, *Hardcreme*. "To maintain stiffness, simply rub on member." I remember the day it arrived quite well because it definitely did *not* come in a plain unmarked wrapper. The brand name was written in blue letters so bold you'd think they were advertising to my mailman. "Maybe he'll think it's furniture polish," Joan said. *Hardcreme* did nothing but turn my "member" a ghostly white. But it did bring me a flood of mail on "related products."

Have you tried *The Splint?* Four dollars. It looks like a doctor's tongue depressor, and you put it on the underside of your penis. "To attach, slip 'part' through rubber loops. Guaranteed to keep 'part' at proper angle." Does it work? I'll never know. I never got my "part" hard enough to push through the loops.

Then there's *The Bumper*. This can be yours for $6 or "no more than a pair of gloves." (I am reading from their literature.) It is made of flesh-tone plastic and is worn at the

HAROLD: *Friday Afternoon*

base of the penis. It looks like a little pink shield with a hole in the middle. On the top side of the hole is a raised "bumper" that is meant to rub against "your partner's clitoral area." Joan said it hurt.

A dildo is an imposing object. The $12.50 version (large) we sent away for looked more like a religious object than a sexual device. The Lord's tool. We have the circumsized version in bubble-gum pink with a realistic touch of blue to the veins. (You could also get it in chocolate brown.) It's hollow and when you slide into it, you feel like a little boy putting on a mask. People commonly think dildos are used only by lesbians. Wrong.

The first time I put on our dildo I was reminded of a high school joke about ugly girls. "I wouldn't fuck her with your dick." It does feel exactly as if you're wearing someone else's penis.

Joan and I had to get a little drunk before trying it, and as I was inserting it she let out a screech of pain.

I'd neglected to grease it.

I put on some vaseline and got it in. Joan had been laughing, but she became suddenly quiet and began working herself up and down on it. It then became my turn to screech. "My balls! The damned thing is cutting into my balls."

Maybe a dildo takes special training, but I was never able to get any sexual feeling inside it, although I liked watching Joan react to it.

The one device that *did* work was really simple: a rubber band.

The idea came from Joan who had read that erections are caused by blood rushing into the penis.

"If you could *keep* the blood inside your penis you'd keep the erection," she said. And it sounded logical.

We got my penis semihard and snapped on a small green rubber band. It stayed semihard. We made love. It stayed hard. Joan came. My penis felt slightly numb, but I was terribly excited. She'd come with me inside her, *hard!* We used the rubber band for over two weeks, but one day I told our urologist about it. The first word out of his mouth was "gangrene."

"*Gangrene?*" I felt panic. My grandfather had lost his leg because of gangrene.

"Yes, you fool. You'll get gangrene with that rubber band if you haven't got it already. He examined me, but I was all right. "You're lucky," he said, "but don't do it again."

Other doctors told us that there was no chance of gangrene or any other trouble from the rubber band. But we'd been frightened to death and could never bring ourselves to use it again.

Along with physical aids, we also used psychological devices—pictures, dirty movies, and once, real people.

The dirty pictures were the usual shots of people doing everything. We'd flip through them together at bedtime, hoping to get me hard. Sometimes I'd lie between Joan's legs, spread a halo of pictures around her head, and rub against her, while looking at them. It didn't work, and made us both feel creepy.

Watching dirty movies together was a slightly better game. We'd strip, turn on the projector, and wait for inspiration. When the movies got us aroused, we'd have oral sex. If you're in the right mood, this can be terrifically exciting and you don't feel too disgraced afterward. Somehow the people in the film always seem dirtier than you.

In Tijuana we tried something that backfired completely. We'd gone down for the Sunday races at Caliente and were lured (it wasn't hard) into one of the *exhibiciónes* that are a town specialty. In a hovel on the outskirts we found ourselves seated on a bench a few feet from a large mattress on which reclined a young, good-looking, nude Mexican girl.

A nude man, about thirty-five years old, entered, and for twenty to thirty minutes they ran through a variety of sexual acts winding up so passionately that they seemed completely oblivious to being watched. It was very exciting for both of us. But for *years* afterward this "entertainment" had a bad effect on me. I became envious of that Mexican. Often, when I'd feel like sex I'd think of him, of how he'd gone twenty or thirty minutes with an erection that stayed stiff as a board. God, how I wanted to be like that! I've heard it said that the men who take part in these acts use special chemicals to harden their penises. But I never really believed it. For me that Tijuana exhibition represented a sexual ideal I could never attain. During the act, we were asked "in," but we refused. I really don't know whether my refusal was on moral grounds or because I was ashamed of the way I knew I'd perform.

JOAN

Saturday Morning

When you commit yourself to spending a fortune for treatment by famous doctors for a serious medical problem, you feel like a complete fool when you don't follow instructions. Harold and I went to the clinic like two guilty criminals.

Dr. Masters greeted us with his usual brisk, "Good morning! Good morning!" and then said, "Tell us about your day yesterday."

So we told them. Actually I did the telling, and I could barely look them in the eyes as I spoke.

"We went back to our rooms," I said, "and got into our positions and did what we were told. First Harold touching me and then I..."

"Yes. Good. And what happened?"

"Harold got an erection again."

"Excellent."

"He was really very excited," I said. "I think it lasted longer than any erection I ever remember him having. We both were excited about it."

"Did anything else happen?"

"No, not at first." I really felt terribly guilty. The plain

JOAN: *Saturday Morning* 95

fact was we'd had sex without permission. We did what we shouldn't have done. So I felt embarrassed and nervous and didn't know what to say. "Harold said he would like to enter me . . . Not really to have sex, of course, but just . . . You know, just . . . Well, anyhow, I let him . . . and then after he entered he got bigger and bigger and bigger until finally he had a gigantic orgasm."

At least I'd finally said it. I couldn't look at either of them. Here I was so anxious for Dr. Masters and Mrs. Johnson to think of us as responsible adults who were serious about trying to cure their problem, and now we'd loused it up. I kept my eyes on the carpet, expecting a big reaction. I got it, but not the one I expected.

"I think what you did was fine," Dr. Masters said. "There's nothing wrong with that." I couldn't believe my ears. "It's wonderful, Mrs. K., the nicest news all week." I quickly glanced up at him to see if he was kidding. He wasn't. He had a great big smile on his face and so did Mrs. Johnson.

"Truly delightful," she said, and nodded her head at me. She must have seen how completely amazed I was.

"We thought you'd be sore at us," I said.

"Oh, no," Dr. Masters said. "You came here so that you'd be able to have normal sex. Well, I hope you're happy about what happened yesterday, because I am certainly pleased. I offer congratulations."

Harold and I felt like singing. If it was all right with them, it was more than all right with us—and it seemed to be fine with them. In fact, they weren't just pleased, they even gave the impression that they *expected* what had happened, and weren't at all surprised.

They could see how relieved we were, and for the first time all week Dr. Masters seemed more relaxed and even a little informal. On the spur of the moment I asked him whether Harold's cure might be coming faster than they expected and if there was a chance we might finish early. He suddenly stopped smiling and got very serious again.

"No," he said firmly, and for a minute I thought he was angry. "Fourteen days is little enough as it is to attack a problem you people have had for so many years."

"Oh, of course," I said quickly, feeling a little embarrassed. Mrs. Johnson rescued me.

"It's perfectly understandable," she said, "that you should feel optimistic after yesterday, but you mustn't rush the treatment. You still have ground to cover."

"As a matter of fact," Dr. Masters said, and I was glad to see that he wasn't angry after all, "your treatment after these two weeks will continue long range from Los Angeles for at least another year. We will have regularly scheduled telephone conference calls involving the four of us, and also we'll want periodic written reports from you."

He then turned to the matter of our instructions, and for the first time all week a certain amount of confusion arose between Harold and me as to exactly what Dr. Masters wanted us to do. Up to then it had all been absolutely clear.

I thought that he said he wanted us to take a complete vacation from sex that day and just enjoy the city. See a movie, drive around, take a walk, have an interesting dinner, just to sort of relax and enjoy being here together.

But at one point, when Dr. Masters and Mrs. Johnson realized that I hadn't had an orgasm the previous day and was still pretty hung up, Harold thought that Dr. Masters had remarked in an offhand way, "Oh, you can satisfy her," but even then we weren't sure what that meant. Did it mean we should try to have regular normal sex? Or that Harold should attempt to satisfy me orally? Or what?

HAROLD

Saturday Afternoon

I've always felt guilty and unmanly if I have an orgasm and Joan doesn't.

Dr. Masters has no patience with this. "If you make it and she doesn't, that's life. The next time will be her turn."

"And what if the next time . . ."

"If you don't satisfy her, it's all right. She'll catch up to you eventually. Don't worry about it."

Or Mrs. Johnson might put it this way, "The idea that people must 'come together' has ruined more nervous systems than anything I can think of."

Nevertheless, when we got back to the room, I felt it was Joan's "turn." Dr. Masters had merely said, If I *felt* like it, I could have sex with Joan. I now know he didn't think it was important, but that day, I interpreted his words as an order to satisfy her. That Joan wanted satisfaction was no secret. For a day now she'd been telling me how aroused she still felt by yesterday's experience. I felt I'd left her in a state of frustration.

The moment we took our clothes off I knew I wasn't going to take a chance on intercourse again. The idea simply terrified me. Although I didn't admit it to myself at the time,

I had a couple of *new* excuses: I'd just done it yesterday and needed time to recover. And Dr. Masters said I could satisfy her in "any manner I wished."

I made up my mind that I'd try to make Joan come orally. "The Third Man" is never a factor when I'm doing that because I know I don't have to produce an erection to succeed. I like it and I'm good at it. I have found that Joan likes me to start gently by skimming her clitoris with my tongue, like a butterfly. Then, as she gets hotter, she likes me to hold it tenderly between my lips and suck lightly on the base. Then, as her excitement mounts, she likes me to alternate between sucking her clitoris and thrusting my tongue in and out of her vagina. At this stage she will often hold my head and rub herself against my face and mouth.

Today, we were doing all these things, but it wasn't working. It seemed to take forever. I really began to get tired. My tongue felt tired. My mind wandered. Finally, she did come, but even that seemed mild. And we really had to work for it. I guess my lack of real passion showed. Joan has often said, "Unless you feel that a man really wants to eat you, really *loves* it, forget it."

And ordinarily, I *do* love it. When we are really into it, an incredible change comes over me. I start to feel that my head has become my sexual organ. As I rub into her crotch with my mouth and face, my head actually becomes like a hard penis burrowing into a dark mysterious place. Sometimes I'll whisper dirty words into her as I eat her, as if sending words into her vagina will cause her extra pleasure. If Joan is in the right mood, these sessions of oral sex can send her into delirious pleasure. I have been able to come simply from hearing her cries of joy, even without having my penis touched by her mouth, her hand or my hand. I just come in the air. When I come like that, the *feeling* doesn't seem to be located in my penis. It's like having an orgasm in the muscles of my jaws or my eyes, or my tongue.

I have a theory that such pleasure from sucking belongs only to impotent men. We have to be able to transform our heads into sex organs because our penises don't work. (Isn't that what happened to Myra when her sexual feelings shifted to her mouth and breasts after she lost all sensation below the waist?)

Even when Joan and I do 69 and I come in her mouth, the feeling is still located in the part of me that is closest to her vagina—my head.

A few years ago, Joan decided that oral sex was a psychological peril for me. She told me that if I'd reached the point where I could be completely satisfied orally, I'd *never* get back to intercourse. After she got that idea, she didn't like being eaten as much. We did it less and less and her responses seemed tamer. That of course had a deadening effect upon me, because my ecstasy is bound up so closely with hers.

Anyhow, as I lay between her legs on that bed in St. Louis, my head had certainly not turned into my sex organ. My brain was too busy wishing that she would come so that "duty" would be done. And when she came I wasn't able to have an orgasm myself. That was all right though, "One for her, one for me" was the way I felt. We were even. I knew it wasn't an ideal situation, but I thought, *I've followed orders and Dr. Masters will know what to do next.*

JOAN

Saturday Afternoon

I like oral sex. Not exclusively as a steady thing, of course, but as a now-and-then change of pace I can have lovely orgasms with it. My only objection, especially in mutual oral sex, is that it isn't very sociable. I mean you're both so busy working on something or other, there's no chance for communicating or anything. I like looking into Harold's face and eyes when we have sex. I like to see his reactions to what's happening. I like to kiss him or talk, to me that's part of the deal.

Oral sex is a legitimate sexual activity, and I hope to enjoy it from time to time for the rest of my life. But that Saturday afternoon in St. Louis when we thought we had a green light from Dr. Masters for Harold to satisfy me, it just didn't work at all. Maybe I was too aroused or too anxious, and maybe I was trying too hard instead of letting sex happen naturally as we'd just been learning that week.

The fact is, we forgot all the lessons we'd learned. The minute we got into the room we undressed and Harold went straight to my vagina the way he had so many times during the early years of our marriage. No romance, no build-up, no tenderness. Not even a little use of the Keri lotion. The

JOAN: *Saturday Afternoon*

whole approach was wrong, and the fault was as much mine as Harold's. He was anxious to satisfy me as quickly as possible, and I guess I was in a hurry to have it happen. We went at each other like two strangers who just met at a party. At least that's how it felt to me. I couldn't seem to get myself aroused to the point of having the orgasm. Which made me feel terrible because poor Harold was working so hard and was so anxious for me to come.

I finally did something I almost never do: I faked it. I was afraid if I didn't we'd either never leave that room or Harold would finally drop dead of a heart attack. I knew I was cheating on myself, on Harold, and on the treatment, but what could I do?

HAROLD

Sunday Morning

On Sunday, the parking lot was nearly empty, and when we got upstairs there was no sign of the staff or of any other patients.

We wandered down the corridors looking for signs of life. "They *did* say seven days a week, didn't they?" said Joan.

Then we heard Dr. Masters. "Hi! Hi! In here." He was waving to us from the door of his office. "Hi" must be his Sunday "Good morning."

We were surprised at the way he looked. He was wearing tan corduroy trousers, a bulky knit sweater, and a pair of white buck shoes. He looked virile, athletic, relaxed. For the first time I realized he was a very handsome man.

It gave both of us a warm feeling to see this other side of Dr. Masters. The Cold Professional almost seemed "one of the boys." As a matter of fact, the atmosphere was so different that *we* began asking the questions.

"Where's Mrs. Johnson?" Joan wanted to know.

"We try to take alternate Sundays off," he said. "I imagine she's home working on the book." They had just finished their second book, *Human Sexual Inadequacy,* and were making corrections on the proofs while we were there.

"Don't either of you ever relax completely?" Joan asked.

"My wife asks the same thing," Dr. Masters said. "My hours must be hard to live with."

"How does your wife stand it?" said Joan.

"She's just faced up to the fact and there is nothing she can do about it," he said.

I felt that he didn't want to discuss his personal situation any further. For the thousandth time that week I found myself wondering about his own sex life.

But I switched the subject to something we'd been curious about since the day we arrived. "Where did you get those pictures in the corridors?"

"Oh, the art collection," he said with real enthusiasm. I'd obviously hit a favorite subject. "Let me show it to you," he said.

The Masters and Johnson "art collection" hangs on the walls outside their offices. It consists of scores of gag pictures that have been sent to them by former patients and research subjects.

"They started coming in right from the beginning," he said. "There's apparently something about this place that turns people into humorists. We began hanging them up years ago, and it must have given new patients the idea. We still get new ones every week."

"After the first book, I received hundreds of requests from people who wanted to become research subjects. They'd even send me nude pictures of themselves. One man offered me a small fortune, provided he could look over his partners first. I also remember a letter from a man who said he was a male prostitute and could take care of twenty to thirty research projects a day for us, and he didn't care what sex he was used on.

"After the first book came out a lot of people were upset by our prostitutes. 'Are you comparing American women to a bunch of whores?' Things like that. It was like Freud being told that his conclusions were all right if you happened to be a middle-class Viennese Jew."

Masters and Johnson had started out with prostitutes as research subjects and got a lot of information from them. But early in the game, they decided they needed more "normal" subjects. They found it was surprisingly easy to get volunteers, particularly college students and their wives. Pretty soon members of the general community were offering themselves for study. So it's nonsense to say their first book is based entirely on the sexual habits of whores.

We walked back to his office, the mood still remaining more relaxed than ever before. He sat down and asked, "How did you two spend yesterday?"

I told him I'd tried to satisfy Joan orally and that I thought she had come.

"I definitely had an orgasm," Joan said. "Not a great orgasm, but an orgasm."

Then I began telling him how satisfied I was with the way the program was progressing. As I talked, I studied his face to see whether he agreed or not. I must have still believed I was being tested for "right" and "wrong."

He seemed pleased with my report.

When I finished, he said a very peculiar thing, "You're doing so well, we really ought to get you a couple of blondes."

"Wha—aat?" Joan was floored. First of all, she's a brunette. Second, she's fiercely jealous. And who could have expected such a remark in the first place.

Dr. Masters kept right on going. "Do you like blondes? Perhaps you'd rather have a redhead. I know some lulus."

HAROLD: *Sunday Morning*

I was every bit as surprised as Joan. I simply couldn't figure out what he was up to. I murmured something about brunettes being all right for me, and that seemed to close the subject.

What *was* he doing? Had I acted smug? Was he trying to put me down? Was it Joan he was after? Or was it some kind of joke? That didn't seem too likely. I felt the remark had a purpose, but as yet I had no inkling what that purpose was. I couldn't have guessed that, with this remark, he was beginning the most important part of our therapy.

Dr. Masters acted as if he hadn't noticed our startled reaction.

"You two deserve a rest," he said. "So here is your next lesson. No sex, no massage. Nothing. Just make believe it's Sunday at home."

We made a date for the next morning and left. As we walked to the car, Joan said, "Blondes!"

Then in the car, she said to me, "If you want a blonde, be my guest." His remarks had really shaken her up.

HAROLD

Sunday Night

We were waiting for a table in the restaurant when Joan suddenly grabbed my arm. "Don't look up, but you'll never guess what I see."

It was another couple from Masters and Johnson. It was the first time this had happened and I felt alarmed. What were we supposed to do? Was it all right to talk to them? Was it forbidden? Could it have a bad effect on our case? On theirs? Why hadn't we asked Dr. Masters about this situation.

As far as I could see, no good could come of talking to them. I didn't want to hear how well they were doing at Masters and Johnson. That might have made me feel we weren't so successful. I didn't want to hear any complaints. That might have made me lose some faith in the clinic. My impulse was to avoid them. But we didn't have a chance. They marched right up to us, introduced themselves as Francine and Al F. They were about thirty-five, from New York, and before I knew what was happening, the four of us were having dinner together.

It turned out to be their last night in St. Louis.

"We're celebrating," was almost the first thing Francine said to us. The word and the way she looked at her husband left no doubt: their two weeks had been successful, and they were bursting to talk about it.

I told them we'd been in St. Louis only one week.

"We're sort of celebrating, too," added Joan who wasn't one to be outdone. I felt as if we were speaking in code. The word "celebrating" suddenly had sexual meaning, like the word "knew" in the Bible.

But there was little need to stick to the code. We were like patients with the same disease who were dying to compare notes. Surprisingly, the idea no longer alarmed me. They were extremely friendly people, and, besides, I was curious as hell to find out the nature of their problem. When the girls went to the ladies' room, I casually mentioned how impressed I was with the clinic. That's all it took.

"It's a miracle," Al said. "I still can't believe that in only two weeks they've cured my premature ejaculation. I thought I'd be stuck with it for life." He looked me straight in the eye as if to say, "OK, that's me. Now what are you here for?"

"I hope they're as good with secondary impotence," I quickly said, and by the time the girls came back to the table, the gates were open. The four of us sat there until after midnight swapping symptoms. It was a pretty wild conversation for people who'd never met before, but being together in St. Louis made it almost as easy to discuss sex as to talk about the weather.

Their difficulty was his nearly total lack of control. "Just being inside her was all it took to make me come," he said. "Maybe I'd last five or six seconds, usually not even that. I'd try extremely slow strokes—that made it worse. I'd try not moving at all. That wouldn't work. I'd strain every muscle in my body trying to hold back. I'd take a couple of drinks first. I'd sometimes masturbate an hour or so before, but even that didn't improve matters much. I'd ask Francine not to show signs of passion, to lie there like a stone. I'd tell her,

'Don't move, don't moan, don't breathe hard,' but nothing could hold me back. The mere thought that I was having intercourse seemed to be enough to trigger me.

"I'd try to think of other things. Crazy things. I'd sing old songs to myself. I tried solving math problems. I'd try to go over every detail of my day. I'd think of sad things like my father's funeral or the time our boy was in the hospital. Once when there was an airline crash in the headlines, I tried to imagine what *that* was like."

By the time they reached Masters and Johnson their marriage must have been almost as bad as ours. "I was so frustrated," his wife said. "I was afraid even to think about sex. We started doing it less and less and that *really* made the problem bad."

"If I'd hold off for more than a week," he said, "I couldn't even last long enough to get inside her. But thank God for one thing. We were able to discuss the problem, not act as if it didn't exist. If it hadn't been for that, we'd never have come here."

I don't think they could have revealed all these details if their situation hadn't changed so completely in St. Louis. Their cure was so dramatic that Joan and I had trouble believing it.

This man who couldn't make love for more than a few seconds was now able to prolong intercourse for an average of twenty or thirty minutes before ejaculating.

The thing responsible for their cure was a method of postponing ejaculation called the Squeeze Technique. Dr. Masters taught it to them by means of drawings and a sculpted model of the penis. For anybody who comes too quickly it sounds like the miracle of the age.

In the Squeeze Technique, just before a man is about to come, the woman holds the head of his penis between her thumb and the first two fingers of the same hand (thumb on bottom). By squeezing for three or four seconds, with fairly hard pressure, she can make the man lose his urge to ejaculate.

"At first," said Al, "Dr. Masters told us to use the Squeeze Technique without having intercourse. Francine was to give me an erection by hand and keep stroking my penis until just before I felt like coming. Then she was to quickly use the Squeeze, wait fifteen to twenty seconds and start over again. The first time we tried it didn't work at all. I came. But by the second day we were able to go for half an hour and seven or eight squeezes without my ejaculating."

He said the trick was learning *when* to squeeze. "Francine had to get there just before my 'point of no return,' to grab me just before that stage when my ejaculation was inevitable."

After two days of using the technique without intercourse they took the next step.

"Dr. Masters told us to have intercourse with Francine on top of me. When I was inside her, neither of us was to move. We were just to enjoy my being there. If I felt like coming, Francine was to raise herself off of me, take my penis by her fingers and squeeze. Then after twenty seconds, I was to reenter her."

"Wasn't not being able to move terribly frustrating for Francine?" Joan asked.

"Actually, it was thrilling," Francine said, "so thrilling I was able to come. I loved just feeling him in there without worrying about whether he was going to come. And by the second day we began moving around anyhow."

After a few days they were able to have intercourse with fairly strong movement for as long as fifteen minutes and they only had to squeeze once or twice each time.

By the second week, Al's control had become so good that Masters had them using different positions. The day before leaving they timed themselves at half an hour before his ejaculation, and she'd only had to squeeze once.

"The only thing we haven't tried yet," said Al, "is the good old standard position. Me smack on top and Francine on the bottom. Dr. Masters said it's the hardest position of all in which to control yourself. He said to try it if we wanted, but not to get discouraged if it doesn't work. Besides, who needs it. The other positions are just as good."

Their story seemed almost too good to be true, but months later when Masters' and Johnson's book came out we found this statement. "Premature ejaculation is the easiest male sexual dysfunction to treat effectively. It should and can be brought fully under control in our culture during the next decade." Right now they have been successful in more than ninety-seven percent of the cases they've treated.

Before we parted that evening, Francine and Al had heard our complete story too, and we traded addresses. "I'd love to hear the final chapter of your story," Al said, "I hope Masters and Johnson have something as good as the Squeeze for secondary impotence."

He hoped.

ST. LOUIS

THE SECOND WEEK

HAROLD

Monday Morning

This was the craziest, most mysterious meeting of the entire program. I think I know now what they were doing, but at the time their tactics left us both confused and angry.

At 9:30 Monday morning, the four of us were in his office. Dr. Masters started by asking whether we'd followed Sunday's instructions.

"Did you really take yesterday off?" he asked.

"No action whatsoever," Joan replied. "We get an *A*."

Then, Dr. Masters was suddenly back on the "blondes" again.

"I really *should* have a couple of blondes for you. Maybe that's what we both need, a couple of blondes."

I was more bewildered than on Sunday.

"You're provoking me, Doctor," said Joan.

"Don't be angry," he said sweetly. "It's just man talk. We men like blondes, don't we, Mr. K.?"

Joan was really getting angry. "You're trying to get me to fight with Harold over an imaginary blonde," she said, "but it's not going to happen. No, it's too damn silly."

"Why?" he wanted to know. "Why is it so silly?"

"Why don't we just drop blondes and get back to his problem," Joan said.

"Maybe you're right," said Dr. Masters. "It's awfully early in the morning for blondes." He really was relentless. "Maybe later," he added.

Then he got off on a new track, one that came as even more of a surprise than the blondes.

"You know it's Monday, Mr. K.? I meant to remind you to call your store in Los Angeles."

The store? *Now* what was he getting at. I hadn't thought of the store in a week.

Joan moaned. "I thought we were going to forget that store of his."

"You simply can't forget the world," Dr. Masters said. "This isn't Shangri-la, you know. You have to keep in touch with life."

"I think his mind should be one hundred percent on the problem," said Joan, "not on that store."

"She's probably right," I said. Already I'd begun to worry about whether Papa had taken care of the burglar alarm system.

At this point, Mrs. Johnson said something that really frightened us. She asked Dr. Masters, "Don't you think we should send them back to Los Angeles for a little while now?"

I felt as if I'd been hit with a hammer.

"Send us *home?* But why?"

"Oh, you can return in a week or so," she said casually.

"No, I wouldn't want to go home now," I said.

What were they doing to us? First blondes. Then the store. Now this.

Then abruptly the mood changed. Dr. Masters turned to Mrs. Johnson and said, "I don't think they have to do that. I believe the situation is well under control."

And that was that. No explanation was offered at the time.

HAROLD: *Monday Morning*

The atmosphere became more relaxed again, but Dr. Masters wasn't going to let us forget "life."

"Don't forget to call the store," he repeated.

Then he had another "good idea." He decided we should split up for the day.

"Mrs. K. could do some shopping," he suggested. And I "might be interested in looking over the furniture stores of St. Louis."

"Each of you do what you feel like today and I'll see you tomorrow." His tone of voice indicated the meeting was over.

"Haven't you forgotten something?" asked Joan.

"What?"

"Isn't there any lesson for today?" she asked.

"I think it might be a good idea if you were to take one more day off from sex."

Walking to the car, Joan said, "Those two must have gone nuts over the weekend."

Looking back, I think this is what Masters and Johnson had in mind that day. They felt we'd been in a "hot house" atmosphere long enough and were trying to create a situation that would bring our life in St. Louis closer to our normal life-style. The "store" certainly brought my mind back to "life." The idea of "going back" made me realize that their support would not be permanent. The idea of splitting up for the day was certainly typical of our lives in LA. The whole unexpected thing confused us and made us edgy and uncertain and slightly irritable. I hoped they knew what they were doing.

JOAN

Monday Afternoon

The business of blondes and phone calls and splitting up Harold and me really had me annoyed. What was Dr. Masters trying to do, rush us into divorce?

I knew, of course, that he was sort of kidding with the blonde and redhead thing, or was he? I frankly wasn't too sure. I mean what *could* I think when I found that Harold took him seriously about the phone calls. Right after we left Masters and Johnson to wash up in our rooms at the hotel before lunch, Harold got on the phone and talked to the store, then to a manufacturer in Portland, then to his father again and then to his mother at home. I sat in that room twiddling my thumbs for an hour and forty-five minutes waiting for him to finish. It was just like old times.

We split up after lunch, and I went and had my hair done. The dryer, of course, burned the back of my neck, and when I got out on the street I found it was icy cold, and it started to rain. I got soaked running back to the hotel because I couldn't find a taxi, then bought a couple of magazines and sat alone in the room reading until Harold showed up.

The evening capped the day. In the rain and the heavy traffic we couldn't find the restaurant we wanted, and Harold started to blame me because I couldn't read the map correctly in the dark and gave him some wrong directions. He yelled at me so angrily that I finally told him to forget the dinner and take me back to the room.

As soon as we were alone in the room we had a fight that was as loud, angry, and bitter as any in all our lives. We brought up everything, throwing all our grievances in each other's faces, hurting as much as we could. We didn't stop for dinner, and even skipped breakfast in the morning to scream at each other some more.

JOAN

Tuesday Morning

By the time we got to the clinic the atmosphere between us was absolutely frigid. I waited in the lobby while Harold parked the car. The receptionist saw me and asked, "Is anything wrong, Mrs. K.? You're not your usual bouncy self."

I sure wasn't. "Men are no damn good," I said. "As far as I'm concerned they can all go to hell."

The receptionist was surprised but didn't say anything, and when Harold came in she told us to go right upstairs. We usually sat in the waiting room holding hands, but this time he went over and sat in a corner and I sat down on the other side of the room, picked up a magazine and tried to read it. Finally the door opened and Dr. Masters himself appeared, which was something he'd never done before. He pointed a finger at me.

"You," he said, "into my office." Then he pointed his finger at Harold. "You sit there. When I'm ready I'll send for you."

I went into his office and sat down, but the minute he shut the door I burst into hysterical tears. I could barely talk. Dr. Masters was surprised and tried to calm me down.

"What happened?" he asked. "Just tell me exactly what happened."

I tried to tell, but I couldn't. I was sobbing and crying so hard my words were incoherent. At that moment, though, Mrs. Johnson came into the room and I managed to get control of myself and tell them what had happened. "Harold was completely in the wrong," I assured them. "And I wouldn't say so if it wasn't true."

"Well," Dr. Masters said. He leaned back in his chair and looked over at Mrs. Johnson. She had more to say.

"Mrs. K.," she said, looking at me in a way she never had before, "we've been sitting here for a week listening to you speak for your husband, and we're pretty tired of it. We think it's time you stopped."

I looked at her as though she was crazy. Where was my sympathy? "What are you talking about?" I said.

"I'm talking about your habit of speaking for your husband. The man has a mouth of his own; he doesn't need you to talk for him all the time."

"You've got some nerve," I said. "Here I've been pushed around by him all night and all morning, and instead of sympathy you're picking on me, too." I forgot my tears and glared at Mrs. Johnson.

"You're here to face the truth," she said. "If we want to know anything from your husband, we'll ask him. You don't have to answer for him. You've been trying to run this treatment ever since you got here, and we've had just about enough of it."

I was stunned and close to tears again. "Well," I said, "he shouldn't do what he does to me," but I didn't trust myself to say more. I wasn't so tough or sure of myself anymore. I guess Mrs. Johnson saw that I was upset because she then spoke more gently to me.

"I'm sure you mean well, Mrs. K., but you mustn't try to

take over so much. Just let Mr. K. tell us his version of things, including what took place last night."

"Do you think I'm lying? Have I ever said anything that wasn't true?"

"No one says you lied. But people have to tell stories from their own point of view. Perhaps accidentally or unconsciously they leave out facts that color something one way or the other. And in any case you shouldn't try to tell us all the time what your husband thinks. He isn't a fool; he can tell us himself. And we can tell whether he's right or wrong."

This was really wild. Why was she going at me? I'd tried so hard all week to do whatever they said. After all, it was my idea to come to St. Louis in the first place. I thought they wanted us to have a good time, to give the visit a holiday-like atmosphere to get Harold relaxed. But I wasn't the one who loused things up; he was. I took all that crap from him in the car and hotel yesterday—and now *they* were giving me hell. And look who was doing it, too, Mrs. Johnson, the one I thought was my friend.

I couldn't understand why they were acting this way. Later, much later, I decided it had something to do with the treatment, like a sudden switch from being nice to getting tough. But at the time all I could think was that Harold would probably get worse from them. I mean if they could treat *me* that way when I was in the right, what would they do to him?

When I went back to the waiting room, Miss Bowen told Harold that Masters and Johnson would see him now. I sat back and nodded my head. Now he'd get his.

HAROLD

Tuesday Morning

It made me nervous to be sitting there without Joan. This was the first time in over a week they wanted to see us separately and I couldn't imagine why.

The receptionist caught my eye and smiled. I was afraid my nervousness showed. *Smile of pity, no doubt,* I thought and tried to look as though nothing was troubling me. You get the feeling in St. Louis that the entire staff guesses your mood from the way you walk in each morning. It's disconcerting to know that if you're holding hands, say, the receptionist is probably thinking, *Ah, isn't that sweet, they're doing well.* Or, if you're not smiling contentedly, they're thinking, *Oh oh, those two are in big trouble again.*

I wondered if the fight was the reason they were seeing us separately. Stupid! How could they possibly have known about it. I found myself getting furious with Joan all over again.

Bitch! She's probably giving them her version right now, turning them against me.

Joan has never once conceded that a fight was her fault. No matter how horribly *she* behaves it's always because *I* was worse, or *I* started it. You can't argue rationally with

Joan when she's mad. You can hardly get a word in edgewise. I get so frustrated fighting with Joan that I begin to get louder and louder. And then she gets louder and louder, and we both wind up like savages.

By now I was burned up with *all* of them. How could Masters and Johnson be so biased as to listen to her side of the story alone. I started re-creating the fight in my mind so I could review my side clearly.

And then the door opened and Joan came out shaking her head and looking as if she'd been whipped. She sank into the chair without even glancing at me.

What in God's name had they done to her? Frankly I didn't feel much sympathy. Just surprise and curiosity. But I didn't have time to ask what happened. I was immediately called into the office. As I entered, both Dr. Masters and Mrs. Johnson looked very stern, but the moment the door closed, they both started to grin like a couple of conspirators.

"You should have been here," Dr. Masters said. He pointed at Mrs. Johnson. "She gave your wife hell."

"Why?" I asked. "Because of the fight we had?"

"No," Mrs. Johnson said, "we had to do it because of your wife's attitude all along. She's been behaving as if she were the third therapist in these sessions. You've been taking the blame for everything while she's been acting like a know-it-all."

They really had her there. I thought of the thousands of times she had told me how "normal" she was, how she knew all about sex, all about everything. "Know-it-all" sounded just perfect. I even felt embarrassed for Joan.

"We like her enormously," Mrs. Johnson said. "You can't help liking her, but we had to set her straight."

I felt I should say something in Joan's defense, but all I could think of was, "She means well." That sounded pretty lame, so I added, "She just likes to talk a lot."

"That *had* come to our attention," said Mrs. Johnson. "Yes, indeed, she can talk. And she's smart too. We just like to hear from you once in a while."

"She looked awful when she came out," I said. I was now getting a very warm feeling for Joan.

Mrs. Johnson said, "Let's get her in here. And remember to be kind. I was pretty hard on her. She may be a little subdued now, but I have a feeling you're going to need earplugs this afternoon."

When Joan walked in, we must have been smiling over the earplug remark.

Dr. Masters said, "See both of you tomorrow *together.*"

JOAN

Tuesday Afternoon

In what seemed like less than a minute Miss Bowen was back for me and said I should return to the office. That seemed awfully fast. As I walked down the hall, I saw the door open and the three of them sitting there, laughing. I realized instantly they hadn't said a thing to Harold the way they had to me. And as soon as I walked into the room they told us we were dismissed; they'd see us again the next morning. I didn't even sit down.

I started to shake a little. These two people obviously thought I was in the wrong. And for all I knew, maybe they believed I was the cause of Harold's troubles, too.

I walked out of the office with my head down, not looking at Dr. Masters or Mrs. Johnson or anyone else as we made our way outside. When we got out of the car at the hotel, I wished time would pass instantly like it does in the movies. I dreaded the fact that I might have to face the possibility that some of the failures could be my fault.

I managed to get into the room and hang up my coat and sit down in one of the chairs with my back to the view of the park. Harold took a chair across from me, and when I finally

JOAN: *Tuesday Afternoon*

lifted my head and looked at him, the tears immediately poured out. I really came apart.

My crying was so uncontrolled that Harold began to get frightened. "Honey," he said, "don't cry. Honey, please don't cry."

But I just couldn't stop. I sat and cried and cried because I knew Mrs. Johnson was right. In spite of all my protests, I really had to admit that I *was* doing something wrong. And I wanted to understand what it was so I could try to stop.

Maybe it was exactly what Mrs. Johnson had said. Almost from the time Harold and I first met, when we were with people and he wanted something described, he'd ask me to do it for him. I guess after a while I did it without being asked. It's my nature to be that way—I'm a sort of take-charge girl. But I really thought I was protecting Harold. To most people he tries to seem able to take care of himself. But I know how this man has suffered, how badly he's been hurt by the loss of the most important thing a man has—his manhood. So I figured he married me, a strong woman, to talk for him and to help him share the pain.

But instead of helping Harold I was hurting him. Instead of being his mouthpiece, I should have encouraged him to stand up to people and speak for himself. Well, I hadn't done that at all. I'd only helped to dig a hole that Harold was sinking into. So my tears kept pouring out.

He'd never seen me like this. I was always the gutsy one, the girl ready to fight back with a punch in the nose or a kick. Now for the first time in our marriage Harold saw me as a vulnerable, very unhappy woman. Our roles were completely reversed. I needed help from him.

By three in the afternoon I finally stopped crying. Harold had helped calm me. I washed, changed my clothes, and we went upstairs to eat. It was an odd hour, and the coffee shop was practically empty. We ordered something and then Harold reached across the table and took my hand.

"I'm sorry about yesterday," he said.

I didn't trust myself to answer because I was afraid I'd burst into tears again. So I tried to tell him with my eyes and my hand on his that it was all right, but maybe he misunderstood my silence. Because then he looked down and said he had a confession to make to me.

"I cheated on you, Joan," he said. "I had sex with a hooker last year."

The tears came again; I simply couldn't stop them. Why did he tell me that? Hadn't I had enough? I couldn't blame him for seeing a prostitute—I'd shut myself off completely. Despite the problems he had, Harold was still a man. He had to have some release. I tried to pat his hand and indicate it was all right, but I just couldn't stop the tears.

HAROLD

Tuesday Night

Why did I choose just that moment to tell Joan about Ruby? Hadn't she been through enough for one day?

Pure meanness, I guess. I knew the story would get her started again. I didn't want her to cry because I didn't like seeing her in pain. But after all those years of her opinions, advice, and penny wisdom, that crying seemed like one of the most *human* things I'd ever seen her do. Somehow it put us on an equal footing.

Not that the Ruby story is very threatening. A little shabby perhaps, but certainly nothing a wife should throw fits about. Actually, it's a story that's hardly worth mentioning, except for the fact that it's sort of funny.

While Ruby really is a whore, she's also a Registered Physical Therapist with an office in one of the new medical buildings on Wilshire. Her name is on the board in the lobby and right there in gold letters on the outside door of her office. She's even got a USC diploma hanging on the wall ("It's genuine! No shit!" she says).

To get a blow job from Ruby, you don't just hand over $15 and lower your pants.

First you have to have a *prescription*.

The first time I visited her I called ahead. "We can give you a four fifteen appointment," a remote voice said. When I walked in, Ruby, a showgirl type, was in the outer office dressed in a white nurse's uniform.

"I've come for the four fifteen massage," I said.

"Do you have a prescription?" she asked. I thought it was a joke.

She went on. "Dr. M., two floors down, will give you one. He charges fifteen dollars for his consultation." Then she broke into a smile and said "his fifteen dollars covers six months of treatment. But *me,* I'm fifteen dollars each. And please make sure you give him your right name."

Ruby must have called ahead, because when I walked into Dr. M.'s office he was already filling in the prescription. "Bad back eh," he said as I walked in. "What was that name again?" He handed me the prescription and said, "Best thing in the world for you."

Back upstairs, Ruby filed the prescription in a metal cabinet. The whole thing was as efficiently organized as IBM.

"Simple safety measure against any possible trouble," Ruby explained. "It's absolute proof that I'm legitimate."

Even then, Ruby doesn't blow you. First she insists on giving you a full massage. Then, as a finishing touch, she says, "I'll vibrate you off for fifteen dollars or blow you for twenty." I chose the latter, and I've been back at most three times. For *that,* Joan exploded.

Ruby is my only slip in all the years with Joan. Loyalty is really my middle name. But I began going to prostitutes about eighteen months before Myra died and continued until I met Joan.

My experience with whores made me realize that I'd become some kind of sexual case. I've never been able to keep an erection long enough to enter a whore. I've got as far **as**

HAROLD: *Tuesday Night*

touching the outside of a whore's vagina with the tip of my penis, but never beyond that. Although I've practiced a great variety of perverse sexual acts with prostitutes, I've hardly ever had an erection while doing so.

When Myra was alive, my secret trips to prostitutes made me believe I'd become a low, despicable person. That in itself contained some solace. When I was unable to get an erection in the presence of a prostitute, I told myself that my guilt was the reason. And my inability to produce, actually made my visits seem less sinful. I remember a prostitute sucking on my penis for over half an hour trying to give me a hard-on or make me come. As she worked on me desperately, I said to myself, "It's better this way." I felt relieved that I wasn't getting pleasure from the experience. (The girl, by the way, stopped after the half hour, said she felt like a failure, and offered to give my money back—the only time that has ever happened to me.)

After Myra's death I was still unable to perform adequately with prostitutes. Now my excuse became "remorse." It was "too soon" to be free of guilt. I thought time would heal me. Or maybe the right whore. But I sensed something pretty serious might be wrong, for even when I'd masturbate my erections were becoming less and less hard. The word "impotent" never crossed my mind. I *had* screwed, hadn't I? I even had a child.

Yet despite my failures, how I loved whores! I was excited by every one I ever went to, and I loved every step of the process that led me to them.

I loved being *told* about a new whore. The information would usually come from Alan P., an old high school pal. He'd say something like "I've got a new one in West Hollywood," and the mere sentence would arouse me. I could hardly wait to call.

I even loved the phone call. Just hearing the girl's voice

would make me hot. So did wondering what kind of face and body went with the voice.

I loved driving to their apartments. In the car, I'd try to decide what kind of sex I felt like. Since I couldn't have intercourse, I was always trying to think up new things to try. Did I want her to lick my entire body? Did I feel like watching her masturbate? Having a whore, you know, is something like owning a slave for a while. They'll do almost anything you want. It seems to be one of the rules of their game, so your imagination can run wild.

The first sight of the girl was almost the best part of all. Ugly or pretty didn't seem to matter. If they were good-looking or sexy-looking, fine, but if they were too fat, or too old or plain-looking that was all right too. Then the experience took on a kind of extra depravity. Also, the uglier they were, the easier it was for me to make "odd requests."

Not that my requests were really so curious. I'm sure my sexual imagination is pretty limited. For the record, these are some of the things I'd do with a prostitute:

> Have her blow me.
> Have her lick my entire body and then blow me. (This is called round-the-world.)
> Have her jerk me off.
> Watch me jerk myself off and let me come on her.
> Have her masturbate while I jerked off.
> Have her masturbate and jerk me off at the same time.
> Have her masturbate and have her use my hand instead of her own.
> Rub my soft penis against her clitoris until she came.

My desire, as you can see, wasn't simply to have an orgasm myself. I wanted to see the girl have one, too. This was a pleasure I hadn't known in years. Thus my delight in watching them masturbate. I realized they might have been acting a lot of the time, but if they were, they were good actresses, and their displays of passion would give me extreme pleasure.

Of course, all those sexual acts with prostitutes were preceded by my sad tale of my inability to have an erection. That brought out still *another* great thing about whores. They always had something cheering or encouraging to say about my problem. They provided wonderful excuses that would convince me, for a moment, that not having an erection was the most normal thing in the world. I still remember many of them:

"You must be tired, honey."
"Maybe you haven't been eating regularly."
"You've been doing it too much lately."
"It's the humid weather."
"Maybe I'm not your type."
"It's going around a lot these days."

My pleasure in prostitutes would, however, turn into terror the moment I left them. Immediately, I'd be seized by an unshakable conviction that I'd picked up VD. Each morning for weeks after any encounter, I would search each part of my body for symptoms. My heart would stop beating if I saw a pimple. Could *that* be a chancre? Is that a burning sensation I feel in my penis? Is that "a discharge" or merely a last drop of urine?

The location of the "symptom" meant nothing. Syphilis, I was certain, could strike any part of my body. Every time I'd see a medical book in a doctor's office I'd instantly turn to the section on venereal disease. I was virtually a walking encyclopedia on the subject. My knowledge wasn't reassuring. "A chancre formed on the patient's eyelid" read one book.

"Chancre on left shoulder." "Infection occurred when patient touched utensil used in nursing diseased relative."

Not having intercourse with the prostitute was no protection either. I was sure that I could get it from any part of the girl's body, maybe even from inhaling her cigarette smoke. Or from my *own* hand if it touched hers.

Not that I ever exhibited a single symptom. There was absolutely no relief in that, though. Have you ever looked into those medical books? Listen to this: "Sometime a symptom may be so mild as to go unnoticed. In many cases there are no symptoms at all."

There was the real stunner. No symptoms! Just wait twenty years for total blindness or paresis. Or if not struck down myself, I feared that my children's children might some day keel over in the street because of my weakness.

Even blood tests (I'll bet I've taken twenty) didn't convince me I'd escaped. I always wanted to tell the doctor, "Shouldn't we peek at my spinal fluid, just to be sure?" It seemed so foolish, I never asked.

But my love of whores always prevailed over my fears. Long before the "incubation period" was up, I'd be back with still another. I'd try to swear off but never could stop until I married Joan. And, as I said, my record after that was nearly perfect.

JOAN

Wednesday

The next morning when we got to the clinic I apologized to Mrs. Johnson for the way I'd talked to her. She told me I'd done nothing wrong.

Dr. Masters asked us what had happened the previous day. I started to answer him, then closed my mouth and let Harold talk instead. He told them what we'd been through. Dr. Masters seemed pleased, especially that Harold had told me about his experience with the prostitute.

"It helps clear the air," he said, "so that nothing stands between you. The basis of a good marriage is trust and honesty, and it's the only way we can achieve positive results with the patients who come to see us."

"Our failures," said Mrs. Johnson, "come from lack of honesty. We had a local couple come to us, and the woman didn't tell us she was seeing an analyst at the same time. Each day we'd discuss the problem and treatment here in the office, working things out together with the patients, coming to certain agreements. But the next day the woman would behave entirely differently as a result of discussing the session with her analyst. The treatment never worked. We have to have honesty."

I thought about that a lot in the hours after we left the clinic. And finally I realized what I had to do. We were out driving somewhere and I asked Harold to park. There was something I had to tell him.

In the early years of our marriage money was really a problem. The furniture business was awful, and Harold was snowed under with debts from Myra's sickness and death. To try to help us along, I took a course in stenography and I got so good at typing and shorthand that I got a job before the course was over. It was with a group of young, bright insurance salesmen who each sold well over a million dollars' worth of insurance a year.

I was their Girl Friday. I typed their letters and kept their records, and they liked me because I was accurate and dependable and never complained about the work. In fact, it soon got to the point where they trusted me to take care of the correspondence. They would just tell me what kind of letter to write and knew that I'd take it from there. And there was usually so much to do each day, that I wouldn't finish my typing till seven or eight at night. They waited around for me to finish so they could sign the letters, and then I'd drop the letters in the mail.

Harold used to close the furniture store at six and then come to pick me up. He'd sit with the boys while I typed, and often they'd play cards in the office until I finished the work. Harold never lost. He's a good poker player, but to this day I think those fellows purposely lost to him. They knew about our financial problems, and their poker losses to Harold damn near furnished the first place we took, so that Harold's daughter could move back and live with us. Barbara was around twelve then and resented me, of course, but I did the best I could with her.

After three or four years, when our debts were paid and

the furniture business improved, Harold wanted me to stop working, so I left the job and stayed home. But I kept in touch with the fellows, and once in a while when they had an emergency they'd ask me to come in and help out.

Later, when Barbara was at college, there wasn't too much for me to do at home, so when they called one day and asked me to help a friend of theirs who'd lost his private secretary, I was glad of the chance.

Owen Dunbar was one of the most brilliant and unusual men I've ever met, the head of one of the country's largest independent brokerage houses. By an odd coincidence, he has a lot in common with Dr. Masters. Both are stocky and forceful, bald and bright, always in control. The main difference between them is that Mr. Dunbar was twenty years older, a man in his early seventies.

But I didn't know that when I went to work for him. Mr. Dunbar ran every detail of his business which was a large one. His company covered six of the largest universities on the West Coast, handled nearly eighty percent of the marine insurance out of LA and San Francisco, as well as most of the biggest banks and aerospace companies. He had the most fantastic memory I ever saw. We called him the human computer, but of course he was much more than that. His interests were so wide-ranging. He loved opera, for instance, and whenever he could, he'd fly up to San Francisco for a performance. He also gave them money. Something else I found out by accident one day as I was looking for something in his desk—he wrote poetry. This embarrassed him because he said a really great American poet was an insurance executive back east, I forget the name, but that's the sort of man he was.

When I went to work for him, I'd been married for eight years, and for a year or more at that time I'd had practically no sex of any kind with Harold. After I'd been on the job for three or four months Mr. Dunbar started telling me about his life, how he was paying alimony to a first wife. After I'd been there for six months he told me his second wife, a very nice lady who was his own age, had given up sex completely several years before.

So I wasn't surprised when he propositioned me. In fact, I was pleased. Mr. Dunbar had a virility that stirred me sexually for the first time in years. I'd almost reached the point where I thought I'd become frigid, and now here was someone who found me attractive and seemed to bring out the woman in me, too. I knew damn well that when I brought him papers to sign I leaned closer than I had to. I often touched him "by accident," and I always wore a perfume he liked. So when he said he wanted to have sex with me I was interested. He was persuasive. I agreed.

On his way to the office one morning he registered at a hotel and brought the key to work with him. He left early for lunch. I followed twenty minutes later and went straight up to his room. He was wearing a robe, and there were drinks and food on a table. Everything very nice. I still called him Mr. Dunbar, and told him about some calls that had come for him after he left for lunch. He gave me a champagne cocktail, and we ate hors d'oeuvres and talked about things in the office. Then there was a pause. Mr. Dunbar looked at me. I knew what he wanted. He'd said so many times in the office that he couldn't wait to see me without my clothes on.

I got up and went into the bathroom. While I was undressing, I found that my hands were shaking. I put on a negligee I'd bought on the way to the hotel and went back inside to Mr. Dunbar. He was still sitting on the sofa. I took off the negligee and let it fall to the floor. He stared at me.

"You're a very beautiful woman," he said. He stood up as I approached the sofa, and his robe fell open revealing his penis fully erect. Now I stared. It was the first erection I'd seen in years.

Mr. Dunbar put his hands on my breasts, and I reached for his penis. The minute I touched it, he came.

I wasn't surprised, I knew how aroused he was and I know how men react. We both washed and put on our robes and sat down to eat some lunch. Mr. Dunbar apologized for coming so quickly like that, and explained he hadn't had sex for a very long time.

"In fact," he said, "this is my first indiscretion in more than twenty years. My last was with my present wife before we were married."

He didn't have to tell me he wasn't a swinger, I knew that for myself. After lunch we tried sex again, and this time he got in me before he had his orgasm. It didn't work for me. I mean I didn't have an orgasm, but I learned at least that I was still sexually alive.

About a week later Mr. Dunbar said he'd like to try again, and he also started to tell me he thought he was falling in love with me. I stopped him right away.

"Mr. Dunbar," I said to him, "I know that in spite of everything I must love my husband. Why else would I have stayed with him through all these years?"

He agreed that I was right and that neither of us should throw away what we had. When Harold became suspicious of the calls Mr. Dunbar made to me at home, I quit the job and never went out with him again. To this day, though, he calls me once in a while.

I told Harold about Mr. Dunbar as gently as I could. But there's no such thing as gently when the subject is infidelity. Harold took it hard, and my heart really broke for him. I knew what went through his head. I'd told him he was justified in seeing a prostitute when I'd denied him my body.

By that token, what were my rights as a wife when my husband had no manhood to give me?

We went back to our room and I fell on the bed, terribly depressed at the mess I'd made. Harold sat on the chair in the darkened room and thought his private thoughts. Finally, he came and sat beside me on the bed.

"Let's try to hold on, Joan," he said. "I'll protect you and watch over you and I won't let anyone hurt you. I promise. I'll stay with you the rest of my life."

This brought me into his arms. It was what I'd waited so long to hear. I wanted so much to be loved, to be number one in Harold's life. For the first time I believed it would happen, that he'd make me the most important thing in his existence. I held onto him the way a drowning person holds onto a lifeguard. He got into bed with me, and we clung together for dear life.

HAROLD

Wednesday

If she'd told me that he made love like a Don Juan, the marriage would have been over for me. I love Joan, but I simply couldn't have survived that kind of competition.

From the moment she began, from the instant she said the word "affair," I was waiting for her to reach one part. *How did he do in bed?* I swear I nearly asked the question. When I heard he'd hardly performed at all, I felt suddenly safe. My marriage had been given back to me. To this day, I carry in my mind a picture of Dunbar taking off a flannel bathrobe and ejaculating as soon as Joan touched his penis with her fingertip. I can feel his embarrassment. I gloat over it.

The fact that he was so old gave me comfort too. I'd met Dunbar, a stuffy-looking man in a vest, with the kind of face that I have always associated with Pasadena money and the Methodist church. I would have guessed him to be fifty-five to sixty. When Joan said seventy, I felt pleased. Seventy made any real danger seem unlikely. She could hardly leave me for a man who'd barely be able to get around in a few years. Even his money couldn't have been an attraction for Joan. She's not that kind. I make enough for her. So when she said, "It was absolutely over," there were lots of things that made it possible for me to believe her.

What *did* make me angry though was that her story wasn't just a confession—she seemed to be bragging about the whole thing. She started out sounding sorry enough, with her "I've got a terrible, terrible thing to tell you" and "This is the hardest thing I've ever had to do." But as she warmed up, I could swear she was *showing off,* as if I was supposed to think she was some kind of deep, sensitive, intellectual type because this "brilliant man" had found her sexy. It was really annoying to hear all those details about his poetry and love of opera and $1,000,000 a year, and the "deep respect" people gave him.

Now that I think of it, she'd always acted that way. When we first met, she'd tell me stories about "previous lovers," and there was always some sort of name dropping going on. She'd never say something simple like, "And then so-and-so made it with me." Not Joan. First you had to hear that so-and-so wrote some damn movie or other, or that his father owned a chain of department stores. There was always some little detail calculated to make me feel about ten miles out of her league. If she ever had an affair with a bus driver, or the gas man, I never heard about it.

When she finished, I wasn't ready to let her stop talking. I still had one major question on my mind: *Had there been others besides Dunbar?*

I admit that I'd wondered about some of "the boys" she used to work for. They, too, she'd always been sure to tell me, had "minds like steel traps" and "such diverse cultural interests." I'd always figured "the boys" would be pretty diverse sexual partners, too. In those days I thought every man except me was "good in bed."

I said, "Look it's out. But before we say anything else, tell me if he was the only one?"

"How can you ask a thing like that?"

"Swear it."

"Of course, I swear it. I never even *thought* about anybody else but Mr. Dunbar."

"If you've got any more confessing to do, do it while we still have Masters and Johnson."

I was convinced she was telling the truth. If there'd been anybody else, I'm sure it would have come out that day. All I had to face was my own reaction to Dunbar.

Curiously, it was my impotence that made it possible for me to live with the fact that she'd betrayed me.

As I sat in the darkened room, I know I wanted to feel forgiveness. I didn't want to lose Joan over this. I didn't want my marriage to end. But instead I turned mean. I called her "whore," "traitor," "cheat." I threatened divorce. I wanted to beat her. I told her that in the Bible adulteresses are stoned to death.

It was all an act. These were merely the things I felt entitled to say. The wronged husband! I was punishing her, but if she'd suddenly stood up and said, "All right, divorce me, it's fine by me," I'd have thrown myself at her feet and begged her to stay. But she just sat and looked sad, and for a while her misery only triggered new meanness in me.

Then I thought of my impotence, and my rage cooled immediately. Suddenly Joan was no longer the bitch who'd betrayed me. My own condition had forced the situation.

I wasn't the innocent victim.

I'd taken part in her sin as surely as if I'd delivered her to Dunbar's bed.

Now I was able to find different words, words of love and forgiveness. I don't know just what I said, but I know that I felt an overwhelming love for her. I'm certain I loved Joan that night more than I've ever loved anyone in my lifetime. We were in trouble, but for the first time it was *our* trouble. Not her trouble. Not my trouble. Our trouble.

JOAN

Thursday

Dr. Masters and Mrs. Johnson could see something new had happened, as soon as they saw our faces. I couldn't wait to explain.

"I told him about Owen Dunbar!"

"Good!" said Dr. Masters. "We both were hoping you would." He and Mrs. Johnson were obviously very pleased.

"It wasn't as hard as I thought it would be," I said, and I thought instantly of what every woman has ever said about giving birth to a child: When it's over, you forget the pain. Telling Harold had been a hard thing to do, but keeping the secret of Dunbar to myself ever since it happened had made me feel worse, even more so in St. Louis. Dr. Masters and Mrs. Johnson had respected my confidence, and of course I was glad they did. But the Dunbar load was heavy, and in spite of the pain of confessing, I was glad to be rid of it.

Actually Harold had taken it better than I thought he would. No man likes to hear about his wife's affairs, it makes him less of a man, and Harold had little enough confidence to begin with. But outside of being angry for a minute or so—probably because I gave Dunbar a buildup as a wonderful person and all—he really seemed glad to hear it in a way. I

JOAN: *Thursday*

guess he realized I was telling the truth that the Dunbar thing was all; there was no other fooling around.

Mrs. Johnson wasn't deceived by my brave talk about not having trouble confessing. She knew I'd suffered and congratulated me for my courage. "It isn't easy to admit you've done something you think is wrong," she said.

That made me feel better. Mrs. Johnson usually knew the right thing to say to me—even that time when she tore into me. I guess it was something I asked for. It just came at such a bad time, when I was expecting sympathy after my fight with Harold, rather than a scolding. Later, of course, I calmed down and realized how right she was.

But this time Dr. Masters topped her. He nodded his head very seriously and pointed the letter opener at us.

"Up to now," he said, "the two of you have been living together as roommates. Well, you've just been married. Now you're man and wife."

I believed it. Harold believed it. And it was hard to know whether our pleasure that morning was greater than Dr. Masters' and Mrs. Johnson's. They both glowed as I know we did, and I had trouble concentrating on Dr. Masters' words as he tried to warn us that we still had work to do. He also cautioned us that day that people might try to ask us for advice when we got home from St. Louis.

"Confession," he said, "can be a good thing for the soul. But you can't just advise people to talk freely about their indiscretions. It could cause more harm than good; the problem's generally more complicated than that."

I realized much later how right he was, but at the time the comment that stuck in my mind was: "You two have been roommates . . . now you're man and wife." That was it. The lies and secrets were over, we'd laid it all on the table. Harold and I had stood in front of each other completely naked, and both of us still loved what we saw.

I barely remember leaving the office when the session ended that morning, but I know my feet didn't touch the ground all the rest of the day as we strolled around St. Louis.

The only worry I had was that Harold would think about the Dunbar business again and get upset. He actually did bring it up once—in bed—but I could see his anger was over. I could have shouted with relief. Instead I said nothing and just gave Harold a kiss.

HAROLD

Thursday

So sex had to be faced again. It frightened me. For three days I'd kept it out of my mind.

On Sunday and Monday there had been no sexual instructions from Masters and Johnson.

The fight with Joan on Monday had made sex impossible.

Her collapse on Tuesday eliminated any thought of it.

Her confession yesterday had ended with real feelings of love, but we hadn't expressed those feelings in sex. Funny, isn't it, that in one of our deepest emotional moments, we didn't think of sex. We actually avoided it, as if sex and love didn't belong together. I remember feeling that way when I was courting Myra. Old Jewish expression: There are girls you fuck and girls you marry.

Perhaps Joan also believes sex and love should be separate. I have a theory that my impotence was one reason she married me. She'd been terribly promiscuous before we married. Once she told me that she'd had more than fifty men. Maybe marrying a man with whom she couldn't have intercourse represented a kind of purity to her. It's a crazy theory, but it makes sense when you remember that her first husband was queer, and that her one shot at adultery was with a seventy-year-old man.

Today Dr. Masters had been quite clear. We were to resume the sexual exercises. Not directed toward any specific goal—just for the pleasure of touching each other.

In his office Joan had taken my hand. It was the first time we'd acted romantically in front of Masters and Johnson. The way he'd said, "You aren't just roommates now—you are man and wife," had so moved us that we automatically reached for each other. What feeling there was in that hand clasp! If we could come close to that in bed, our problems would be over.

We mooned around downtown St. Louis the rest of the morning like a honeymoon couple. We even bought a small gold heart that came in two pieces like a jigsaw puzzle—one half for Joan, the other for me. When the two pieces are joined, you get a message. Ours read ETERNALLY YOURS.

I didn't think of Dunbar again until that afternoon when Joan and I were in bed, our bodies covered with the lotion, and Joan's hand on my penis.

It hadn't become hard, but I was in ecstasy from her stroking. Then Dunbar appeared in my mind—a picture of him sitting behind a large desk dictating a letter to Joan.

I had no erection to lose, but my feeling of pleasure disappeared. One unexpected thing did happen, though. I was able to tell Joan about my fantasy.

"Guess who I just thought of?"

"I suppose it's inevitable for a while," she said.

At least it's an honest answer, I thought.

"I'm glad I was able to say it." More honesty.

She kept fondling me, not saying anything. The atmosphere remained strained for a while, but soon I could feel the pleasure she was getting from touching my penis. I forgot Dunbar and let myself get very hot.

That night at dinner we laughed a lot and were very hungry, a sure sign we'd been happy in bed.

It must have been that night that Joan said, "I know the sexual thing will be okay because we have so much time to work on it."

She didn't mean that we had a lot of time at Masters and Johnson. She meant that our marriage was going to last. It had been so long since we'd dared think that.

JOAN

Friday

I remember once hearing Truman Capote say on the David Frost show that true love is when you can feel satisfaction and fulfillment with someone without the necessity of sexual orgasm. Well, that was Thursday night. We'd caressed each other with love and Keri lotion, and though we didn't try to have sex we were satisfied without it.

The glow was still there on Friday morning. I held tight to Harold's hand as we entered the clinic. I watched his face with love as he explained to Dr. Masters and Mrs. Johnson how well it went for us the day before. But I thought to myself that love is even better *with* sexual satisfaction, and I wondered if we should try for another "accident." The last one had happened very casually, and Masters and Johnson hadn't been upset and angry the way we worried they'd be. So maybe, I thought, maybe they really want us to experiment on our own without any actual instructions. The important thing, Dr. Masters had said at the roundtable, was that sex is a *natural* function; he stressed the word natural so much. Well, the natural step after a man has an erection and the woman's excited, is to put the penis inside.

The day before, when Harold was lying on his back facing

me and I manipulated his genitals to an erection, I'd thought of straddling him and getting his penis inside me. It looked so inviting. And then it would have been easy for us to slide into the nice sideways position we used for the accident the previous week. Why not try that tonight?

Before we ended the session, though, Dr. Masters returned to our personal relations.

"It's great to see you two holding hands," he said, "but only saints go through life like that, and I don't know any saints myself. All of us have problems, things we can't control. You two are bound to quarrel. *Everybody* quarrels. But I beg you both, don't let quarrels become the pitched battles of the past—or even the one this week."

I held Harold's hand tighter and said, "We'll never fight like that again. In fact, we may never fight."

"Oh, you'll fight again," he said. "Just don't let it become Armageddon."

We knew what he meant. Harold asked him a question that was bothering me, too. "What can we do about it? We never mean to let our arguments get so bad that both of us begin to bleed. But somehow or other they do."

"Well, one of our couples told us about a signal they invented to stop themselves before trouble."

"A signal?"

"In their case I think it was a word. But it could be anything—a whistle, a wink, a gesture—even something silly. The point is, don't let the battles get bloody."

Dr. Masters had mentioned the idea of the signal sort of casually, but I liked it and thought it was worth a try. Harold and I discussed it as we wandered around the city that day.

"Why not 'trolley'?" I said.

" 'Trolley' what?"

" 'Trolley' nothing, just plain 'trolley,' that's all."

"It's as good as any, I suppose," Harold said, "but why the word 'trolley'?"

"To remind us of St. Louis—the trolley song, remember?"

Harold smiled and shook his head at my logic, but we shook hands and made it official. The magic word was "trolley."

Back in the hotel room we took baths, and then watched TV together, lying in bed without any clothes on. As we watched, we also idly made love to each other, and even before we used any of the lotion, Harold had an erection.

It was lovely. We were just sort of playing around with each other, but somewhere in the back of my mind I felt we had a chance for something great to happen. We were in the process of making love the way normal people do. We were kissing and fondling each other, enjoying each other's bodies. This was going to be the complete and perfect sexual act.

And then the damn telephone rang.

HAROLD

Friday Night

It was my brother on one extension and my father on the other and they were both talking at once, but there was no doubt what they were saying.

"Mama may be having a stroke, and we're trying to get her into a hospital." Could we come home fast?

"Has Dr. Shulman been there?" Yes.

"How serious does he think it is?" They weren't sure.

"Can I talk to Mama?" No.

"Can she talk to anybody?" Not too well.

It took all my nerve to ask this. "Are you keeping anything from me?" It had suddenly hit me that Mama might be nearly dead and they couldn't bring themselves to tell me.

"No, no. We're **telling** you everything." My brother sounded truthful. "It **may not** be bad, but call Dr. Shulman now, anyhow. Then call **us back** and tell us what you're going to do."

"We need you now, Buddy." It was Papa and it was the first time he'd used that nickname in years.

I told Joan what had happened while I dialed Dr. Shulman.

Dr. Shulman was calmer. He said he thought she might be

having a stroke and that he was going to see her the next morning.

"Is it serious enough for us to come home right away?" He wasn't sure. There would have to be tests.

"It's not a matter of life and death, but . . ."

I told Dr. Shulman we'd be on an early plane and that we'd call him from the airport. I hung up and called TWA for reservations. Then I called the desk and told them to have our bill ready. Then I called Los Angeles again. My brother still sounded rattled. He and his wife always fell apart in emergencies, always relying on Joan and me whenever there's trouble. When I heard that shaky voice of his, I wondered if we shouldn't try to leave tonight.

"No, you don't have to do that," he said, "and listen, here's a surprise for you."

Mama was on the phone. Her voice was so weak it frightened me. But she made her little joke. "Harold, don't worry. I won't die until you get home."

"Joan and I love you, Mama," I said. And she repeated, "I'll live until you get home."

When we hung up, I told Joan I talked to Mama, and she cried with relief. Then she turned to me and said, "Maybe we should call Dr. Masters?"

"*Dr. Masters!*" Fifteen minutes before, Masters and Johnson had been the center of our lives, now I'd nearly forgotten them. It was as if the whole experience had dropped into a well. It seemed unreal, foreign, pretentious, almost silly.

"Forget it," I said. "We'll tell him tomorrow. We'll have plenty of time. The plane doesn't leave until one."

Actually, Dr. Masters had flashed through my mind when I'd made the reservations. I remember thinking that we'd still have time to say good-bye if we left at one.

"I think we should tell him now," Joan insisted.

HAROLD: *Friday Night*

I said I didn't want to talk to Masters or Johnson or anybody.

I noticed we were both still covered with the lotion.

"I'm taking a bath," I said. "And get rid of this damn stuff."

I was getting angry. Our nudity seemed especially inappropriate.

The bath calmed me down. First I tried to think of Mama, but instead I found myself going over what I'd say to Dr. Masters and Mrs. Johnson the next morning. My warm feelings for them began to return. What had happened in St. Louis didn't seem silly anymore.

Joan came in and stood nude by the tub.

"It makes Masters and Johnson seem kind of unreal, doesn't it?" she said.

"Just for a moment," I said, "they're real again now." Seeing Joan there, I knew I hadn't dared test myself sexually since that one moment almost a week ago. I wondered if that was enough to go home on.

JOAN

Saturday

The first thing Dr. Masters said when he heard we were leaving was, "You should have called me right away."

"We thought about it," Harold said.

"In fact, we almost had a fight about it," I added. "But we didn't have your number, and besides it was pretty late. We didn't want to disturb you."

"I never consider a call from a patient a disturbance," Dr. Masters said. He was upset that we'd be losing two sessions, but of course he was sorry to hear about the illness. He also asked how our day went yesterday and was very pleased to hear that it was good.

"You people are very close to success," he said. "That's why I'm a bit sorry you have to miss these last two sessions."

"It won't really spoil things, will it?" I asked.

"Oh, no," he said, "nothing can stop your cure. It's only a matter of time." That made me feel a lot better. Dr. Masters was surprised to see that I was relieved. "Come on," he said, "you both know the progress you've made here. I'm not giving you news. Sure, the cure isn't complete—it may take a year to achieve, but I promise you that by the end of that time, and maybe a good deal sooner, your sex life will be entirely normal."

JOAN: *Saturday*

In a way, I shared his confidence, because I knew how well it went the night before until the telephone rang, but I just prayed that leaving wouldn't spoil things.

Dr. Masters stood and shook hands with us, then Mrs. Johnson put her arms around me and we embraced. I was afraid I was going to cry. Even though she'd been rough on me that one day, I understood now that she did it because she felt she had to, and for all the rest of the time she was warm, sympathetic, and understanding. I was grateful to her, to both of them, but I didn't know how to say it. So I just didn't say anything, and I've been sorry ever since. The last thing Mrs. Johnson said to us is something I think about often.

"The two of you have so much going for you," she said. "I knew it from the first day you came into the office."

I hated to leave. St. Louis had been a refuge from all the troubles of our normal life, and Dr. Masters and Mrs. Johnson had become like wonderful friends. And I wasn't sure we could manage things on our own again. But Dr. Masters seemed to read my thoughts because the last thing he said to us was an important and reassuring reminder.

"The four of us will continue to have telephone conferences at regular intervals. And if you ever have an emergency, call me at any time. I don't mind being disturbed. Understand?" We both nodded. "Good. Now don't forget to stop in at Miss Bowen's office and make your first telephone appointment."

Miss Bowen gave us a card telling us to phone at eight o'clock in the evening on Tuesday, February 24. We left the building with a trail of good-byes from the people on the staff.

The minute we started for the airport my mind leaped straight across the country to Los Angeles. We were going home to a mess, I could tell that from last night's calls.

Harold's brother was weak like their father, and he was married to a shrew. They spent most of their time worrying about whether others were getting more of something than they were. And trying to plan anything with them and the other members of the family always wound up in fights.

Thinking about this made me shudder, and I remembered Dr. Masters' advice on that subject. I hoped we'd learned something in St. Louis that would help us behave better when the good times turned sour. . . . The screaming and hurting were awful, and I was afraid we were coming back to some of it because of Mama's illness.

Harold interrupted my daydreaming as we sat down in the plane. "Strokes, if that's what it is, aren't always fatal, are they?" Poor Harold's mind was in LA already, too, and he needed reassuring.

"Of course not," I said. "Remember President Kennedy's father? He lived for years after a stroke."

"When I talked to my mother last night," Harold said, "you know what she said to me? I didn't tell you."

"What?"

"She said, 'Don't worry, Harold. I promise I won't die till you get home.' "

Oy . . . That's how Jewish people can behave sometimes. And I can say that without being anti-Semitic because I'm more Jewish than most of them. I mean they're Jews by accident of birth. I actually asked for it; I converted to Judaism.

I got the idea at first because I wanted to please Harold, although he was only a Jew in name himself. His parents were orthodox, but neither of their children was interested in religion till I came along. I guess I realized that the way to reach Harold was through the old folks, and I thought my conversion would help.

I wanted to make it a surprise, so I went to a rabbi in West

JOAN: *Saturday*

Los Angeles instead of the one at our neighborhood synagogue. I told him I wanted to convert and he asked me why. When I gave him my reasons, he turned me down flat. He said he didn't think I was sincere about the whole thing. When I started to argue, he told me he was very busy and would I please excuse him. How do you like that? I was very insulted. And when the same thing happened with a second rabbi, I really became annoyed.

"What's the big idea?" I asked this second fellow.

"The big idea, my dear lady," he said, "is that we Jews are not really interested in conversions. I'm sorry."

"Why not? I don't believe you," I said. "What about Sammy Davis, Jr., and Elizabeth Taylor?"

He smiled a little and shook his head. "I don't say we turn people down completely," he said, "but we do discourage them. And we certainly don't go out looking for customers. We have to be convinced a person really wants to convert before we let him do it."

When a third rabbi turned me down, too, I went quietly to the neighborhood guy who I'd heard was nice and told him my whole sad story. He tried to talk me out of converting just as the other three had, but by this time I knew all the arguments and had a few of my own about why I should be accepted. I finally got him to say he'd help me with one "if." At the end of the period of instructions, if either of us wasn't satisfied, we could call the whole thing off. I said that was fine with me and we started to work that day.

He taught me the history of Judaism and enough Hebrew so that I could read the language. Then he urged me to come to services in the temple on Friday nights and Saturday mornings. To do this, I had to tell Harold what I was doing and give up the surprise. He was so amazed that he came to the lessons with me to see if I was kidding, and then his daughter came, too.

After three months I'd learned all the basic prayers and the do's and don't's of the religion. The rabbi was satisfied and so was I, and he arranged for me to go to a *mikvah,* the ritual bath whose purpose is to cleanse away all of a woman's dirt.

I was carefully watched by a woman attendant as I took a ritual hot bath and then a ritual hot shower. I was then draped in a sheet and taken to another room where I stepped into a small pool. Our rabbi, a second rabbi and Harold came to the doorway, and three prayers were recited. At the end of each, I ducked underneath the water.

Later, when I'd dressed, the rabbi gave me a document which certified I was now a Jew and registered with the United Synagogue of America. We each drank a glass of wine.

On the way home Harold leaned over and gave me a kiss on the neck and then made a terrible face.

"Ugh," he said, "you taste like you came from the ocean."

No wonder. To make certain a woman is thoroughly cleansed in the *mikvah,* the pool is heavily laced with kosher salt.

A few months after my conversion we were married for a second time. This one was a religious marriage in our own backyard under the traditional canopy. Harold's mother and father never got over the whole business, especially the fact that I turned out to be the only one in the family who kept a kosher house.

That was a good time in our life. Well, now we had another. And this one we wouldn't let sour. I looked at Harold sitting beside me on the plane as we neared LA, staring out the window. I took his hand. He turned and gave me a smile.

HAROLD

Saturday Afternoon

I was wildly optimistic—convinced I'd just spent the most worthwhile two weeks of my life.

It's pretty hard to explain, when you think about it. After all, what had we *really* accomplished in St. Louis? I'd been able to raise a few erections. I felt fairly sure I'd be able to get others. But we'd only managed to have intercourse once, and that was almost by accident and didn't last for more than fifteen seconds.

We hadn't been taught any special tricks like the Squeeze Technique. We certainly hadn't accomplished anything as dramatic as Francine and Al's cure. Yet I felt as confident now as they seemed to feel that night we'd had drinks together.

I wasn't even worried about missing the last two days of treatment. Dr. Masters hadn't made a big deal of it and seemed surer than ever that we were going to be okay. I also knew we could talk to them by phone any time at all, and that gave me the sense that they were still treating us.

But I knew the real treatment had already taken place. They'd told us over and over again that I wasn't the real patient, and that Joan wasn't. "The real patient is the marriage." I'll bet Dr. Masters said that ten times. As I sat in the plane listening to Joan recalling her conversation, I realized that things between us had changed completely. I wasn't scared of divorce. I wasn't scared of Joan. I wasn't—knock on wood—even scared of sex. I was only scared that the plane might crash. For the first time in years it seemed possible that I had something to live for.

LOS ANGELES

AFTERWARD

JOAN

The First Few Days

      Harold asked me to call the doctor from the airport, while he collected our luggage.

The doctor's first words were, "Something has happened, Joan," and my stomach turned over.

"Oh, poor Mama," I said.

"She's here in the office. I've just examined her," the doctor said. "She's had a stroke and may soon have another. I want her in the hospital as quickly as possible."

"She'll die," I said.

"She may not with proper care."

"I meant when she hears she has to go into the hospital. She's very afraid of that."

"I know she is, that's why I want you to tell her. She feels most comfortable with you. The only thing is, I'm going to have a little trouble arranging for a bed. The hospitals are all jammed up right now. So I'm sending her home with your father-in-law."

Harold and I went straight from the airport to Mama and Papa's house, where Mama put her arms around me and burst into tears.

"I'm sorry I spoiled your trip," she said. "You came home early for me."

I tried to reassure her that everything was all right, but I was very upset by the way she looked. Her face was pale and drawn with fatigue. Before I could talk to her about the hospital, the apartment filled with relatives who only made matters worse by telling Mama she was going to be fine, that all she needed was rest.

"If the doctor thought anything serious was the matter," my sister-in-law said, "he'd have thrown Mama right into the hospital, right, Joan?"

"God forbid," my father-in-law whispered, looking anxiously at me. I couldn't say anything, so I just kept quiet. Mama needed to lie down and rest, but as long as there was company she felt she had to stay up and talk and make sure everyone had coffee and cake and fruit. Harold and I kissed her good night and said we'd be back in the morning. We hoped the others would take the hint and leave quickly, too.

The next day Mama looked a little better, but she still complained about the headache. Again the house was full of relatives and I couldn't seem to find an opportunity to tell her she'd have to go to the hospital. The doctor called and said he'd have a bed either by three in the afternoon or first thing tomorrow morning. He asked me if I'd told Mama she had to be hospitalized and when I said no he warned me, "You'd better tell her so it won't be a shock. This is a very sensitive old lady with a history of heart trouble, Joan."

He didn't have to tell me; I'd known Mama for ten years. I'd also known that damn family for ten years, too. In order to talk to Mama alone, I'd have to throw everyone out of the house or take her into another room. In either case it would start such a stink about my "taking over," that Mama would die of the racket. But the only way to tell her about the hospital without scaring her too much was to do it gently, by speaking quietly to her, woman to woman.

When I told Harold what Dr. Shulman had said, he told

JOAN: *The First Few Days*

me he'd parked our car right downstairs in front so he could take Mama to the hospital the minute a bed was available. Then he asked me, "Have you told Mama yet?"

"No," I said, feeling a little guilty. "I couldn't with all this crowd."

"What are you talking about?" he asked me angrily. "What if Shulman calls and says bring her over right now? How are you going to tell her?"

"If that should come up, I'll face it."

"If you face it like that, you'll kill her. What's the matter with you? You had a simple job and look how you've loused it up. Can't you do anything right?"

"Well, you've got nerve. Here I'm trying my best to be careful and not start a fight with your family—which surely would kill your mother—and look what I get for my trouble!"

We were sitting together in a corner of the living room. We had started out talking in whispers, but now we were getting louder and angrier. An old-fashioned fight was starting. Except this time I suddenly realized what was happening and I thought of Dr. Masters. Harold was asking me something in that angry tone of voice, but instead of answering, I put my hand on his arm.

"Harold, hold it a minute," I said. "Look at what we're doing. This is exactly what Dr. Masters warned us about. Please let's stop right now."

Harold hesitated and stared at me, the angry frown still on his face. Then the anger turned to thoughtfulness and he nodded his head.

"You're right," he said. "I'm sorry for the way I talked."

We kissed and held each other's hands for a minute, then I took his mother aside and had my talk with her. Later Harold started laughing and came over to me.

"Why didn't you use the signal?" he said. "I thought you were going to say 'trolley' if we ever had a fight."

I laughed, too. "I couldn't remember the signal," I admitted.

By Monday afternoon Mama was in Cedars of Lebanon and getting a series of tests. Harold and I had a choice then. We could stay at the hospital and wait for reports from the doctor, although there might be no answer for days. We could sit up all night and worry about what might happen. We could open a bottle of whiskey and forget our troubles in drink.

We turned down all those ideas and just went to bed together.

HAROLD

The First Few Weeks

I was relieved to get Mama into a hospital bed. I was praying that Dr. Shulman didn't think her condition was as bad as we feared. And I was exhausted.

When we got into the house that night, it was the first time we'd been able to relax in days. We got into bed, both so tired that we clung to each other.

Joan had behaved like an angel for two days, and I told her so.

We were clasped together, nearly asleep, when I felt myself get an erection. Joan felt it against her and put her hand down and started to stroke it. We were facing each other. Joan lifted her leg over my side, and we were in the same position as that day in St. Louis. I could feel my penis throbbing in her hand. She moved her vagina next to it. I thrust forward and felt it go into her. Joan gave a little cry and started going wild. So did I. She couldn't stop herself from moving on it.

"I can't stop! I can't stop. I'm coming! I'm coming!" And I felt her orgasm along the entire length of my penis. I held it inside while she was coming and then began moving in and out of her. I kept moving until I finally came, too. My semen seemed to flow from me for longer than ever before, and Joan seemed to be in another world as I kept emptying myself into her.

Still inside her, I fell into a half sleep. Joan shook me and said, "It works. It works."

Next morning I couldn't believe it. It made the one in St. Louis seem like nothing. Here was everything I'd ever imagined sex could be. And it had happened to *us*.

"Let's call now," said Joan. "I've got to tell them."

I didn't want to. They'd said to wait two and a half weeks and now I was more anxious than ever to go by their rules.

I still thought it was a fluke, an accident, a result of some odd kind of emotion that had been brought on by the two tense days at home.

All I could think of was trying it again, and that night we didn't even wait for dinner. At 6:30, we were undressed and rubbing each other with the lotion. We faced each other on the bed—same as last night. I played with Joan's breasts and she stroked my penis. At first we were probably too conscious of what we were trying to do, but it started happening again. I got hard. I forgot I was testing myself. I could feel Joan slip her leg over me, and then I was inside of her again, with an erection that felt like a piece of steel. I didn't last as long. In less than thirty seconds I started coming violently. I didn't have as much fluid as the night before, and I didn't come for as long a time. But it stayed hard down to my last thrust and Joan said, "Wait, wait. Keep it there." And, still inside her, I could feel her coming.

Two days in a row! That hadn't happened in our entire marriage or courtship.

The next night we failed completely. She rubbed me, but I didn't even get a semi-erection. But I was sure that we had nothing to fear. It was no fluke.

The appointment to call Masters and Johnson was still two

HAROLD: *The First Few Weeks*

weeks away. We thought of keeping a sexual diary so that we'd be sure to remember everything that happened. I'm sorry now that we didn't, because in that two weeks my cure—if it can be called that—took shape.

We were able to have intercourse three or four times. Once I came so quickly it hardly counted. But I also came deeply inside her and fully erect.

We tried oral sex a couple of times, and I came in her mouth with my penis erect. That hadn't happened for years.

During her menstrual period, she made me come by stroking my penis with the lotion. Again, I came, erect.

We also had our failures. I'd become distracted when Joan was rubbing me and lose my erection and not be able to get it back. Sometimes the store or Mama would worry me. Sometimes I'd worry that my sexual recovery would suddenly stop. Then I'd try to *will* an erection, something Dr. Masters had assured me was impossible.

One night we practically went through a word for word replay of our pre-Masters and Johnson sex. It was scary. My penis had gone down, and I found myself saying in that old pleading voice, "Suck it a little, it may get hard." It didn't work of course. But instead of the old feeling of shame, we just shrugged it off.

Now we felt the failures were exceptions. The desperation about sex had disappeared. That was the biggest change of all.

JOAN

The First Six Months

At eight o'clock in the evening we telephoned St. Louis and spoke to Dr. Masters and Mrs. Johnson. The minute I heard their voices I could close my eyes and think we were back in the office. Dr. Masters was very businesslike, and Mrs. Johnson was loaded with charm.

They asked about Harold's mother, and we said she was still in the hospital. We then reviewed our sexual experiences since leaving the clinic two and a half weeks before. They were very pleased to hear our report.

Harold had been having almost no trouble about erections. Occasionally when he did, I'd notice that his eyes were closed. I thought I remembered Dr. Masters telling me at one of our sessions that I should get Harold to open his eyes and look at me and my body. In any case it worked. It was usually enough to straighten him out.

In the first six months after St. Louis we spoke to Dr. Masters and Mrs. Johnson by phone three times and wrote them one letter. They told us we covered by phone what we missed by leaving St. Louis early. Although Harold and I have continued to have our quarrels—Dr. Masters told us during one phone conversation, "You people don't need a

JOAN: *The First Six Months* 171

therapist, you need a referee"—our sex life has gotten better and better. Since they are mainly interested in our sexual problems, our phone conferences have been less frequent.

Within eight months of our visit to St. Louis, Harold's impotence was no longer a problem in our lives.

HAROLD

The First Six Months

We quickly learned we weren't the only people in the world having sexual difficulties.

My brother Milton and his wife could hardly wait to find out what happened "back there." The very moment the four of us were alone, Milton asked, "Exactly what *is* that place? What do you *do* there?"

I was telling them some things about St. Louis when my sister-in-law said, "I think you better not continue anymore."

"Why?"

"I can see Miltie's tongue is hanging out of his mouth. He's drooling."

"Why drooling?"

"Because he wishes we had the money to go there."

Joan and I were shocked. Miltie and Grace had plenty of troubles with money and their kids and with our family. We knew they fought a lot, but it hadn't entered our minds that they were having sexual troubles.

Joan said, "We'll gladly lend you the money and make arrangements for you to go if you're really serious."

If he was serious, Milton wasn't talking.

"Don't be crazy," he said. "We don't need that kind of thing." Then to Grace, "What the hell do you mean *drool-*

ing?" He was sore. She'd let something leak out in front of "the kid brother."

Our friends Jack and Bernice kept asking us questions about how much time sex should take.

"Do they teach people to come together?"

"How long do they say an average fuck should last?"

"How long should you stroke each other?"

"Can they teach you to hold it?"

"Can they make a woman come quicker?"

I guess Jack thinks he's coming too quickly and maybe Bernice isn't coming at all. They still haven't completely leveled with us on that score. And God knows, I've given them plenty of opportunities by practically telling them every detail of my trouble.

Most men, I found, behave like "fellow sufferers" when they hear I've been to Masters and Johnson. They rarely go into details, but I have the feeling that ninety percent of them think their sexual performances are below par.

They are so happy to find *me*—maybe the only man they know who openly admits he's not a sexual athlete.

Every place you look these days, especially in dear old LA, you see men desperately trying to look like studs, with their leather fringes and their boots and their shirts open to the waists and their tight crotches. And who knows, maybe a lot of them are sexual stars.

But what a great service for mankind it would be if some other men went around with signs on their backs saying,

"I ejaculate too quickly."

"I can't always get a hard-on."

"I can't make my wife come."

As a person who's been through it, believe me, one of the worst tortures is the feeling that you're all alone with a terrible secret.

Homosexuals used to suffer in secret, but they seem to be

able to speak out now. The sexually imperfect must outnumber them a thousand to one.

A sexual problem isn't something to be ashamed of. It is not what used to be called a "social disease." It should be as easy to say "I am impotent" as "I've got a cold."

It's taken me eleven years to find that out, and I still haven't learned my lesson perfectly. While I've spoken candidly about my impotence, you'll notice that I haven't told my full name. And, if I didn't think I was at least partially cured, I guess I couldn't have told the story at all.

I'm a man without enough education to know much about psychology or medicine. But I have some ideas why St. Louis worked for me.

One reason, I think, is due to luck.

Masters and Johnson were the first therapists to believe my impotence came from what happened to me with Myra, not from my childhood or my mother. They realized that her sickness had made me hate touching the female body.

By luck, their treatment begins with exercises in touching and appreciating the body. So I was immediately focused on just what was troubling me. All their patients start with these same exercises, but you'd almost think they were tailor-made for my case.

I really can't believe that all their talk about "natural functions" or "uninvolved partners" or the Third Man would have been as effective if I hadn't first been able to get over my queasiness about touching the body.

Even their idea of using lotion seems made for my case. Since Myra, I had always been repulsed by the liquids made by the female body. The lotion masked the moisture and made it easy for me to approach the body with love.

Masters and Johnson didn't try to *blame* either of us for what had been going on. Joan and I had been to plenty of therapists, and they all had talked "blame." One of us was always "a little to blame," and the other was always "a little more to blame." It was like a contest to discover whose fault it "really" was.

Well, Masters and Johnson put a stop to that. With them, *we* had a problem. *We* had to cure it. I stopped playing the helpless victim. Joan became an ally instead of a judge.

When we left St. Louis, I'd been afraid that Dunbar might become a sore spot. But he has actually helped the marriage. Joan's confession has given us both the nerve to be truthful.

They also taught me not to be in awe of Joan's sexual powers. I can still see Dr. Masters pointing at her saying *"You,* you know nothing about sex." This will sound very corny, but I feel that in St. Louis we were like a pair of children learning about the birds and the bees together. Her past experience with men, which had always been a threat to me, finally became unimportant. And my lack of sexual experience no longer seemed to be a disadvantage. For the first time, we were sexually even.

People constantly want to know if they can read Masters' and Johnson's new book and then help themselves at home.

If you have any sexual worries, read that book immediately. *Human Sexual Inadequacy* discusses premature ejaculation, impotency, orgasm problems of women, painful intercourse, sexual problems of middle and old age. The book may not straighten you out overnight, but it will certainly tell you how to start to help yourself.

You will also learn that you are not alone. Masters and Johnson estimate that half of the marriages in America are in sexual trouble and that the great percentage of these people can be easily helped.

That's really the biggest thing we learned in St. Louis: Just because you have a problem, doesn't mean you have to stay that way.

HAROLD

Now

It's not a sex life you'd write about unless you knew what it was like before. It's enough to make me feel normal, potent, manly. In my case it's like a miracle.

Now I can ask for things in sex without feeling like a pervert. "Suck me" doesn't mean "maybe *that* will give me a hard-on." It means I'm dying for it. When I go down on Joan, it's not to do her a favor. It's because I'm dying to do it.

Now, just inserting my penis into her gives me pleasure. I love the softness of her insides as I first slip in. Before Masters and Johnson I could never appreciate that part of Joan. I used to just shove it in, and pray I'd stay hard.

Now, I can hold my penis deep inside Joan's vagina and let her come up and down its entire length. Before, I didn't let myself feel pleasure in my penis. If I did, my erection would go away.

Joan always claimed that she could have an orgasm in seconds if the mood was right. Now I believe her. I've got inside her and felt so hot that both of us have come in a few strokes. Before, if I'd come fast, I'd feel ashamed and she'd turn away.

There's a certain place inside her we call the pocket. When

HAROLD: *Now*

my penis hits it, I can feel her move differently, sort of shift gears. She starts to go wild, to moan, to rub herself against me. This stimulates me even more because I know I can make her come. Before Masters and Johnson I'd get frightened by Joan's smallest sign of passion. Her slightest moan could make me go soft, not because it distracted me but because it set up a demand I couldn't fulfill.

Now I realize that *my* sexual excitement gets her excited too. Before, I felt that she was only accommodating me. Now I feel free to move parts of my body that I used to hold back in sex. I let go with my arms, legs, mouth, all of me.

Now if I lose an erection—and sometimes I still do—I don't feel like a failure. Or if I come and she doesn't, I don't feel like a selfish bastard. I have faith that the next time it will be different. Before Masters and Johnson, I believed things would only get worse.

There are plenty of bad nights, plenty of fights, plenty of times when sex doesn't work, plenty of times when I'm not gentle or she's cruel. But it's a good marriage that will last. I wouldn't have dared say that before Masters and Johnson.

JOAN

Now

Now I can sometimes have an orgasm from him sucking my breasts. For the first time since I was fourteen or fifteen, my breasts are really sensitive. I owe that to Masters and Johnson.

Now we'll do it in the middle of the day. Maybe he'll be working on his photography hobby. I'll rush down and tear my clothes off, and we'll do it right on the cellar floor. Impossible before Masters and Johnson.

Now we can plan it ahead of time. I'll say, *let's do it after dinner,* and he'll still be able to get a hard-on. Before Masters and Johnson, just thinking that he'd have to have a hard-on would keep him soft.

Now I'm not inhibited as I used to be about asking for it. I'll go brazenly over to him, nude, if I want it. If he doesn't pay attention, I'll still take the risk. Before Masters and Johnson I had to be chased. Now I'll lay my head right between his legs, or I'll take his two hands and put them on my breasts. I never would have done it before Masters and Johnson. I used to feel if I asked, I was vulnerable, letting down my barriers. I feared he'd think I was a wanton. Now I just tell him I want to get laid.

JOAN: *Now*

Now I can have an orgasm on my side, on my knees, from behind. Before, I had to have a man on top of me during intercourse. Who knows, maybe by next week we'll be doing it swinging from the chandeliers. Since Masters and Johnson I never know what to expect. We're always trying something new.

Now we'll do things we used to do a lot, like oral sex, or masturbating, or other things. But we don't go to bed and say we're going to try such-and-such. It just comes up naturally in the middle of some wildness.

Now I love it when he comes in my mouth. It has to be something I am focused on, that I want to have happen. And when I do, it feels marvelous.

Sometimes when he slips inside me it's like someone put a hot poker in there. I've never experienced that with anyone else. It's so hot it can make me come immediately.

We have found what we call the pocket. It's inside of me somewhere, and when his penis reaches me there, I can go completely out of my mind. That's the place we try for a lot. I can't really describe an orgasm, but when he hits the pocket, I really come hard!

They say an orgasm lasts only seconds, but afterward there's a sweet feeling that stays with me. I get warm around my waist and hips. I want him to stay inside me, that's the most wonderful part of all, that lingering feeling when the two of us are together afterward.

Now I can talk or yell or even laugh when we're making love. Before Masters and Johnson, I used to have to be very quiet. If I said anything it would break the spell because he was concentrating so hard on getting an erection.

Now I know he can deliver so I can get hot just looking at him. One night we were eating dinner with some friends and Harold kept making love to me with his eyes across the dinner table. When we finally got into bed, just touching me was enough to make me come. I was that eager. Before Masters and Johnson I'd never really be ready because I knew he couldn't come through.

He's a normal man now, so I feel I can criticize him without destroying him or hurting his feelings. That's an enormous relief.

It's not always perfect. Don't get that idea. Sometimes I don't have an orgasm. Sometimes he doesn't have an erection. But instead of going into a sulk, he'll say something like "goofed again." We know it's not a permanent condition like it used to be.

If anyone had told me when I was a kid that my sex life would start when I was forty, I'd have called him a mental case.

Yet that's exactly what's happened. And I know now, months after leaving St. Louis, why we saw couples in the waiting room of the clinic who held hands and couldn't take their eyes off each other. The same thing happened to Harold and me. We left St. Louis more in love than at any time since we met.

I can't really explain how and why it happened. I've tried. I've told, as accurately as I can, what happened those two weeks. But I'm sure Masters and Johnson did a lot of subtle things that were over my head, and that they manipulated us without our realizing it. One thing was made quite clear to me, though, thanks to Mrs. Johnson: I tried to run the show too much. Well, I've changed. I'm not exactly a shy little wife now who walks three steps behind her husband, but you can be darn sure I think twice before I open my mouth. That's a hard thing for me to do, but I try.

Another big thing was Dr. Masters telling me to forget everything I thought I knew about sex, and then showing

Harold and me how to enjoy each other's bodies so completely.

And maybe most important to me is that I'm finally having sex with the man I love. That's a very big first. I never had true sex and true love together before. Take it from me, it's fantastic.

One last thing. Masters and Johnson show in their book, *Human Sexual Inadequacy*, that sex can continue with pleasure for couples even into their eighties and nineties. So I'm looking forward now to forty or fifty years more of it . . .

My husband should live and be well.